Hello To Self
Irvine
Meet
CalJah

Irvine "CalJah" Lewis

Hello To Self Irvine Meet CalJah

Authored by Irvine "CalJah Lewis ©Irvine Lewis2023

Edited by Marcia M Publishing House Editorial Team

Cover Design by Marcia M Publishing House

Published by Marcia M Spence of Marcia M Publishing House Ltd. West Bromwich, West Midlands the UNITED KINGDOM B71 on behalf of Irvine Lewis.

ISBN-978-1-913905-36-1

A copy of this publication is legally deposited in The British Library Archives.

www.marciampublishinghouse.com

Thank You

There are so many people I am so grateful to for their input into my life during my time of illness. It is treasured and invaluable. Some of them I knew, but a greater number I didn't know, but they prayed and helped to make a difference in my journey back to life. I have made my request to the Lord that all of you receive blessings; something tangible that will enhance your lives for the love, sacrifice, advice and support you gave to me and my family.

I could not possibly mention you all, however, I will mention a few significant ones.

The contents of this book are a recollection of the author's journal and memoirs. Most of the character names are pseudo names used for anonymity.

My Family

To my wife and family, you are one of the main reasons I am alive, and it keeps me going. I realised how much I loved you all when the threat of not being able to express that love through death was real. That was not an option—I will live to see you thrive.

To my wife: how did you do it? Looking after me, the children and working full time? You were the one who took action and gave out the information for people to pray. You have been on the roller coaster ride with me from the beginning. When I gave up, it was your faith in action that pulled me through. You are more than gold; God gave me the best that is you.

I've learned so much from you all and I'm still learning. I really don't know what I would do without you guys. You are the best part of my life. Love you all.

Mum and Dad

Thank you for bringing me into existence and leaving me an example of "living life and living it good".

Mum, although you have already gone on before, I thank you so much for your example of faith. You were told you would never walk again, paralysed from the waist down, but you defied the odds and began to walk again after the Lord told you that you were healed. The consultant had to reconsider his observation and prognosis notes because you were not meant to walk again, but you did.

Dad, you too have gone on before, but I thank you for your prayers. You were a praying machine keeping all of your children and grandchildren in prayer. You would pray for hours, and I certainly felt the difference after you left. I felt that I was out in the cold. But you have left me the example of praying without ceasing and laying down prayers for the future generations, like you have done for me and my siblings.

My Siblings

My four brothers and eight sisters, I love you all beyond words. The love and support I received from you all in caring for me and my family is immeasurable. Just being there was enough. You were there from the outset, standing in the hallway of my house within minutes of hearing the news. I had a stroke, consistent and constant in prayer. God has blessed me with a beautiful family. I am fortunate to have you all.

Jo Hall (deceased)

I did not have a clue of how to get the support I needed from the Department for Work and Pensions (DWP), but you helped me until I was successful. The help was invaluable and was in addition to what you and the rest of my siblings were already doing on my behalf.

Caroline Kerr and Monica Lumbsden

While my wife was running twice daily up and down the motorway to see me, you cooked meals and fed my children. Your sacrifice is notable. Thank you so much.

Neville Clarke

Thank you, my brother and good friend. You were the one who initially put the information out, a call for prayer, and it escalated and went viral. If you had not done this, I would not have had so many people interceding for me in prayer to be made whole. Prayer works. You were there supporting my family by keeping the information flowing.

Bethel Lighthouse (BLCC)

Words cannot describe the prayers, encouragement, and help I received from you all. You looked after me and my family, cared for us and still do. To my church family, thank you all. I mention a special thank you to Mother Thompson and Mother Brown, who called weekly to check up on my wife and my progress. I value all the acts of kindness.

Jenny Pinnock

Thank you so much for advice and guidance. You persisted with me to make sure I made the effort to get the support I needed. While I was still in denial about being seriously ill, I tried to be independent. I told everyone I was fine but, in reality, I was struggling. If it was not for you, I would not have even considered all the support I could get to help me get back to work, and get support for my family from the DWP. You didn't just tell me once, but you followed it up every time you saw me to get it done. I did not want to be told a third time, so I got it done. The support was invaluable.

Carol Gordon and Faith Wilson

You both fought spiritual battles for me, kept me in prayer, and interceded on my behalf. You were there in support until I recovered. Those things that you spoke into my life were fulfilled. I was amazed how God used you both to help on my recovery journey. There was a time when I was on the brink of giving up, but I prayed and said, "Lord, I don't feel so good today; you have got to help me and send someone to lift my spirit." Shortly after I gave up, I began to see my life pass before me, but the Lord answered my prayer, saved me from death and sent you both. You prophesied into my life and lifted my spirit.

Michelle Bennett

You were another spiritual watchman and discerner; you interpreted my dreams and gave sound advice to family on what to do. My family took your advice and made sure they consistently prayed until I recovered. It brought my family closer together, and we saw the power of prayer in operation.

Rob and Julie Embury, Darren and Maxine Barlow

I love you guys and I am totally humbled by your selfless acts of love and the support you gave to us. You looked after our son, taking him to training and to his matches when I could not. We did not need to worry about him, and you consistently did this for about two years. Who does that? You guys were amazing, a godsend.

Darren, when I wrote off my car, you took me to work until I was back on my feet.

What you all did for me and my family was very much appreciated and will never be forgotten.

Bethel United Church of Jesus Christ and Other Church Faith-Based Organisations

You are too big to mention you all. I was totally humbled by your concern and the sacrifices you made on my behalf. I could not believe people from the whole organisation and other faith-based organisations were looking out for me in prayer and fasting. Thank you.

Work Colleagues

You guys are one of the best when it comes to friendship, care, jokes, laughs, and teamwork. During my time off work, you sent me little encouragement messages on my wage slip; you did not forget about me. When I was back at work, you allowed me the time to get back into the swing of things, even though it took longer than normal. You came looking for me around the building when you thought I was not well. All you have done for me collectively has meant a lot.

Taxi Drivers

If it was not for you guys, I would not have been able to get to work, take my boys to and from their training sessions. You were a godsend. I've had so much fun, jokes and laughter with

Ablewell Taxis. I met so many new people, all with stories to tell. I learned so much about what's going on in my town from you all; you are better and more accurate than the newspapers!

Hospital Teams

I can't thank you enough. You know who you are, who performed the surgery and who looked after me before, during and after surgery. I am here, alive, to tell the tale.

Brain Tumour Support Group

Thank you for all your support and help. Although I didn't attend many sessions, what I received was enough to help me come to terms with my condition and made me realise I was not alone.

MM Publishing House

Thank you for your invaluable support and guidance throughout the process of writing and publishing this book. Your expertise and handholding throughout have been fundamental in making my vision a reality pushing me past the fear boundary.

To the Most High God

I thank God, the Most High, Yahweh, for my life, your favour and blessings. Lord Jesus, you surely got my attention through illness and took me on a journey of recovery I will never forget. My faith has grown, and I have drawn closer to you. I believe the work you started in me is ongoing, but you will complete it.

Introduction

I'm writing this book, but it's a journal really, of my recovery journey from an illness that took my family and I by surprise. Even though there were telltale signs, I totally missed some and dismissed the others.

I was overwhelmed and amazed by the power of prayer over my life. So many people took time out for me. I realise how powerful and important your mind is, especially when applying consistent, positive thoughts. It can bring you out of many dark situations with optimism when you feel all hope is gone. Equally, the opposite is true: negative thoughts alone can shorten your life.

The challenge for me was to live again! Despite my serious illness, I didn't just want to be alive. I wanted more – I wanted to thrive. Having a near-death experience, I saw things and went to places through out-of-body experiences that I could not explain, but it made me become more aware that there is more to life than the eyes can see. Who are we really? We are more than just flesh and blood.

The whole experience was humbling and caused me to have a different perspective on life and what's really important. I make the most of life and enjoy each day I am alive.

In my recollection of events, I may have missed some information or put some in not in a chronological order. There is also a bigger and much wider picture that I am not aware of; my wife and others would need to fill in the gaps, probably in another book. For those who know me, I apologise if I have missed out any key information. For now, this is how I recall my journey, taken from the journals I kept along the way.

Chapter One
Locked In!

I t was very, very cold; the coldest December on record for 100 years. The temperature would drop to anything between -10 to -20 degrees Celsius overnight. That evening, December the 18th 2010, was no exception; the temperature had already begun to fall. Most nights along my street, the traffic is heavy. I rushed home from work to my warm house. It's always hot. If the children were all at home, it's most likely all the lights at the front of the house would be on too. I hurried home so I could leave early to get to sound check on time for once. I had a gig that night.

As I approached my house, I flicked the car indicator to turn right onto the gravel drive, slowing down to a gradual stop in the middle of the road in parallel to the drive entrance, waiting for a break in the oncoming traffic to quickly turn in.

The approaching car was not moving very fast, so I quickly turned into the drive and lined up the car close to the hedge, leaving room for my wife, Del, to park her car adjacent.

The children were all at home from school, and as usual, the front of the house glared with the brightness of all the lights being on. They were all hungry. Del was still at work. She is a social worker. I could not do that job; it's too stressful for my liking. I would cook that night while Del was at her work Christmas do. It was going to be something quick and easy, like pie and chips, so I could get away early for sound check.

The front door clunked shut, the side window on my right looking into the porch rattled. I said loudly, "Hi you lot! I'm home," in my humorous way. I walked down the hallway past the stairs on my right and the front room on my left straight towards the living room. I switched the hallway light off while passing.

The living room door is always kept open with a doorstop so, at a glance as you walk past, you can see everyone in the room. They all turned their attention towards me, away from the TV, in unison as I passed. Amaris, Reco, Ryan and Miles all replied, "Hello Dad." My youngest, Miles, shouted, "What are we having for dinner, Dad?"

"Pie and chips."

"OK," they all muttered, turning their attention back to the TV.

I walked straight past the living room, through to the dining room into the kitchen, and put the quick and easy meal into the oven. I was conscious of the time.

4

I made haste to double-check my saxophones, freshen up and change into the stage outfit the band had agreed on wearing a few days earlier. I had my ears plugged into my HTC phone, listening to the set of songs we were to play that night. One member of the brass section was not going to be there, as he was rehearsing for his other band, who were performing their last gig the next day. I needed to make sure I got my parts right, as any mistakes would be more noticeable with fewer members playing.

With the children fed and watered, I checked the time. "Oh no," I moaned – I was late again. I packed the car, said goodbye to the children, ran out of the house and joined the long queue of traffic heading towards Birmingham, where the venue was. I did not eat anything, but got two bottles of Lucozade along the journey. The last time I ate was lunchtime, and it was now 8 p.m.

I left a message for Del: "Hi Del, I'm on my way to the venue. The kids have all eaten. Make sure you get there for 10.30. Enjoy your works do. See ya in a bit. Bye."

I also left a message on the bandleader's mobile: "Hi Bradley. Sorry, I'm late – you know the score. I'll be about half an hour late. I'll get there about 8.30, yeah. Cheers."

The venue was not easy to find, hidden in the maze of streets in the Digbeth area. It started to rain. I stopped in the middle of the road to unload my musical gear. The weather had taken a nosedive; the rain had turned to sleet with a very icy breeze. I noisily unloaded the gear into the reception area, then headed back outside to park the car.

I wondered if Del, my work friends and siblings, were going to come. By then a statement was on the radio news, requesting drivers not to venture out in their vehicles because of the severe weather conditions – and that it would become worse.

"Last to sound check again," I sighed, as the guys had already started going through the set. "Hi guys," I shouted with a smile, but feeling quite embarrassed for being late. They responded either with a nod or raised arm as they continued to sing or play. I found a spot to unpack my saxes and set up, ready to get on stage and join in with the rest of the band.

The band was twelve members strong; it's not very often you come across a band as big as that. There was Bradley the drummer, Nelson the bassist, Greg the lead guitarist, Christie, Denise, Tina and Barry the four vocalists, Ben the percussionist, Roy the pianist, Neil the trumpeter, Sonny the trombonist and me, the saxophonist. We played covers of popular RnB, soul, funk and some jazz numbers. We were, essentially, a funky RnB band.

Bradley the bandleader was our drummer and arranger. Nelson was our bass guitarist, Greg was our rhythm guitarist. Roy, the keyboardist, was only a teenager, but a very accomplished musician. Ben was our percussionist; Sonny, the trombonist, was a professional musician and had played for many professional bands. He could do a mean solo on the trombone.

Neil the trumpeter was already in a successful band but loved what we were doing and wanted to be a part of it. Christie was one of the vocalists, petite, with a bubbly personality and lots of energy. She knew how to get a crowd going.

Denise, a professional singer, only a few years before had her own band climbing the Top 40. She has a fantastic voice and is a songwriter and vocal arranger. Tina was the newest member and a very sweet solo singer.

Barry, the only male vocalist, really complemented the band.

On stage, the drums are in the middle of the stage at the very back, with the bass and guitarist on either side of the kit. The keyboards are to the left, in front of the bass, but behind the percussion rack. The brass section is also situated to the left of the stage, next to the percussion rack at the very front. The four vocalists occupied the front right of the stage.

The stage was compact, so it was just as well that there were only two brass members, Neil and I, otherwise we would have struggled to fit everyone on.

After climbing onto the stage, I put my bottles of Lucozade down in front of me. "It's gonna be a long night," I thought, as we started going through the set.

"Arrghh!" I moaned as I got my part wrong. I made an excuse: "My right hand is still very weak and slow; I'll have to improvise my way through." For some time I had noticed how, while in the past I would learn things very quickly without difficulty, now it was hit or miss. It mainly occurred when I needed to use my right hand, and it had gradually got worse over the year. Lack of practice, I thought, not realising the seriousness of what was happening to me. I was already weak on my right side; I could not lift my right leg fully, so my leg was dragging when I was walking. "Ill-fitting shoes!" I convinced myself, and bought some boots instead, which actually helped – my right leg did not seem to drag so noticeably.

After sound check, the band members all went home to get changed and freshen up. "See ya. We're going to get something to eat before we come back," shouted Denise with the rest of the vocalists. I stayed at the venue; I did not want to go out again, even though I was hungry. Besides, I was already dressed. I buttoned up my coat, re-wrapped my scarf, finished my Lucozade, put my woolly hat on, and decided to explore the venue.

The venue used to be an old manufacturing unit that had been converted into a club. The entrance was like a small cubicle with security doors. There is a reception window with slide shutters. If you wanted to get in the venue, you pressed the buzzer on the thin window ledge, and someone would appear from behind the slide shutter requesting the entrance fee. I went in free as a band member. The security doors opened to let me in.

Once inside the foyer, there was a very wide corridor which led to a set of double doors into the auditorium, where we did our sound check. The stairs led down to a bar area with scattered tables. Next to this room was an open doorway leading into the dance hall with a spinning globe in the centre of the ceiling. Next to the DJ booth was a statue of an alien with big, oval eyes. It had a dark green jacket on with a black shoulder bag going across its chest, with an imitation cigarette in one hand, and a drink in the other hand. Each hand only had three fingers. *How peculiar*, I thought. The statue's presence was intimidating, with a dominant effect in the room. I didn't like the atmosphere in there. I was glad to know the gig was not going to be in that room. It was definitely a dark atmosphere.

The place was empty. No one was in the bar or the dance hall and there was no music playing. It was about 10.30 p.m. "How does this place make any money with nobody here?" I said softly to myself. "I hope my family and friends can make it in this weather," I muttered. I did wonder if the gig was going to be a waste of time. As I was heading back into the bar area, I noticed some pictures on the far wall, went to look at them, and the owner of the venue, Tony, came over and started talking to me.

"We don't normally start until 1 a.m.," he said in patois.

"Oh, is that why nobody's here yet?" I replied. "I have told all my crew to get here for 10.30 p.m. We were told that we would be on stage for 11 p.m.," I said, expecting some explanation as to why there was such a contradiction in information.

"Well, there would normally be a support band on first at 12 a.m. for one hour, then you guys would come on at 1 a.m. After that, a DJ would take over. Most people turn up at 2 a.m."

"2 a.m.!" I repeated. I could not see my crew staying that long, especially my work friends; they would probably go home before the band got on stage, at that rate.

He said, "I have changed it up for tonight. You're going on at 11 p.m. because there is no support act."

I went back upstairs to the auditorium to see what was happening. There was no one about, so I made my way back to the car. I turned on the ignition and put the heating on full blast, made myself comfortable and waited for the heat to reach my bones. I fell asleep.

After about twenty minutes, my eyes opened wide as I could feel the atmosphere change in the car to the same feeling I had when I went into the room where the alien-looking dummy was. I looked at the time: 11 p.m. I switched off the ignition and headed back to the venue.

The heating was off in the auditorium. I sat on one of the few stools in the room. The venue was for standing room only, by the look of it. A few friends of Bradley had arrived, then my sister Naomi with her husband Rick. We greeted each other. She asked, "What time are you on and where's everybody?"

"We are supposed to be on at 11, but the rest of the band are not back yet. I can't see us going on until about 11.30 p.m.-ish at the earliest," I replied.

"We have to go at 12," Naomi said.

"OK. It's good you could make it, though; I really appreciate it."

More people started arriving, including some of my friends. My work colleagues texted me with their apologies that they could not make it because of the bad weather.

"You guys took your time," I said loudly to the band members, who were back all dressed up. They burst through the doors, bringing a warm, lively atmosphere with them. We all headed for the changing room, where we always prayed together before going on stage. That night was no different.

"Listen, I know there are not many people here, but we are going to play like we are at the Jam House, OK?" Bradley said firmly.

"OK, let's do it!" we all replied with varying delayed responses.

The auditorium was still fairly empty when we got on stage, which I guess was down to the extremely bad weather. We got into position and started the set. "One, two, three, four," Bradley shouted while clapping his drumsticks together. We went straight into The Brand New Heavies track 'You Are The Universe'.

The audience started shouting and cheering, and gathered more closely around the stage.

We were to play two sets of forty-five minutes each with a fifteen-minute break; each set had about nine songs. The set started about 11.50 p.m., almost one hour late. After the first set, we decided to do all our tracks back to back to shorten the time.

Without eating since lunchtime, I was very weak and jittery. My last bottle of Lucozade was keeping me going. The second set had begun, and we decided to do each track back to back. I did not have the time to rejuvenate with swigs of Lucozade.

I began as a result to feel weak and hollow inside; it took a lot of effort to concentrate on remembering my parts.

In anticipation of the next song, I went to change my soprano for my alto sax as quickly as I could. In doing so, as I leaned over to make the swap, I felt like collapsing. It took all the strength in my body to stay on my feet. I was desperate for another swig of Lucozade, but there was never enough time between songs to get a drink.

There was a solo for me to perform in one of the tracks near the end of the set.

"Concentrate, concentrate!" I tried to focus. I wanted my solo to be perfect, and it had gone well at sound check. The groovy, syncopated brass lines were spot on leading up to my solo. The first part felt and sounded fantastic but, as I went into the second part, all of a sudden my concentration had gone and my memory felt as though it had been erased, like pressing the reset button on a computer. It was blank.

Even now, I'm curious to know exactly what I actually played when my mind went blank. I definitely played something. However, it was not the well-rehearsed solo. I can only believe everyone thought it to be a burst of inspiration on the spur of the moment. I needed that Lucozade as the energy from my body was draining away fast. Just before the last two tracks, I managed to get a few good gulps, after which I felt much better and completed the set without any further mistakes.

The gig was over, and we had some good reviews from people who came up to us while we were packing the gear away. The temperature had dropped considerably to minus seven degrees; I have never known it so cold. After taking Neil home, Roy and I stopped off on Broad Street for a bite to eat. There were hordes of people coming, going in and out of the various clubs, pubs, and restaurants, despite the weather. There was about three inches of snow. It was 2 a.m. on Saturday morning. I got home for 3 a.m. and crept into bed and fell asleep within minutes.

Later that morning, my phone went off about 8.30 with a text message. Ryan, my second son's football training, was cancelled as the ground was frozen. *Great, just Miles now*, I thought. Del was still sleeping, and I fell back asleep again. About two hours later, Del's phone went off with a text message. She picked up her phone, looked at the message and turned towards me and muttered, "Mile's football training is cancelled – the ground is frozen."

"Excellent, I'll get a lie in today, the first in months," I said. I still had one more commitment to cancel: the boys' drum lessons. I went back to sleep.

At 12:30 p.m. I forced myself up and made a phone call to the drum studio and cancelled their drum lessons. When this was done, I exhaled; I could relax for once. With no intention of getting up, I went back to sleep.

At 1 p.m., I gradually started to wake up. Del and I were having a conversation about what we were going to do that day. At exactly 1.15, I watched my right hand start to curl into a fist involuntarily. At first, I thought I was doing it, until I attempted to stop it. It kept curling up tighter and tighter. I thought the bones in my hand were going to break. The pain I was feeling was unbearable, but the more I tried to fight it, the more pain I felt. To the point my whole arm started to shake.

I shouted, "Del! My hand is curling up and I can't stop it."

She took one look at me screamed, "Oh my God!" She grabbed the phone and ran to the landing in shock and blind panic – she was hysterical. What she saw was the whole of my face on the right side had dropped, my eyes were rolling, my speech had gone, my right arm and leg were curled up. I felt my eyes flashing and total confusion in my mind. My teeth were grinding against each other. I was dribbling from my mouth and my whole body was shaking on the bed. She had seen this before with her dad, so she knew I was having a stroke.

In all of this I could somehow still see, in flashes, and hear what Del was doing. I shouted to her out on the landing, "Stop panicking. I'll be all right." What she heard were grunts; my speech was incomprehensible and I might as well have been a dog barking. Yet, to me, I knew what I was saying. I could only see the room in flickers of images while my eyes were rolling. It was enough information to know what was going on around me.

I was locked in! Imagine being locked inside a small capsule (my body) looking through the windows (my eyes), seeing and hearing everything, responding, talking, shouting as you would normally do, but no one can understand what you are saying. I was pressing all the buttons of this so-called capsule but nothing was working! I couldn't communicate with the outside world. In my mind, I was fine, but my body was not working. I could not express myself any more. If I had died, that would be the point of separation; my flesh would return to the earth and no longer exist, but my spirit (the real me) would go to its eternal destination. It was such a surreal moment when I was conscious of two parts to my existence: the physical me, all twisted in the bed, and my mind still thinking, seeing and desperately trying to communicate with the outside world but locked in or trapped inside my own body.

I was in that condition for about thirty minutes or longer, in real time, but to me it seemed like five minutes. Del came back into the room after getting instructions from the paramedics to put me into the recovery position, which was to roll me onto my left side. I did not want to lie on my left side and somehow managed to roll onto my right. At that moment, my whole life passed before me.

I said to myself, *it's not my time yet to die; I have still got a vision to fulfil that the Lord has given me*. Many years ago, I had a vision. It appeared to me three times about my destiny, to fulfil my purpose in this life. I have been pursuing that vision and had not reached it yet.

I also recalled from a distant memory a preacher saying that you can heal yourself by speaking the word in the name of Jesus. This gave me inner strength and courage. I spoke out loud. To the listener it was grunts and groans, but I knew what I said: "In the name of JESUS! Sickness, I command you to leave my body NOW!"

At that precise moment, everything went still and quiet, like an elongated pause of silence. My body stopped shaking, my contorted face went back to normal, and so did my arm and leg. My eyes stopped rolling and, lastly, my speech came back. I gradually gained back control of my own body. At that moment the paramedics arrived and stood against the bedroom wall by the door entrance and asked, "Can you talk? Are you all right?"

I said "Yes," with a lisp. "But I'm speaking with a lisp," I commented. The more I spoke, the clearer and better my speech became. Initially, it was upside-down, back-to-front gobbledegook.

One of the paramedics took my blood pressure, which was sky high, and checked my eyes. "Can you get yourself dressed?" he asked. "You need to go to the hospital."

"I think so," I replied.

My right arm felt like a heavy, gigantic flipper. I could not feel my individual fingers or elbow and could barely move my arm, let alone know where my fingers were to control them. It felt like a big, moveable lump sticking out of my shoulder. It took a tremendous amount of energy and effort to move my arm. I might as well have run a marathon or spent five hours in a gym. However, the more I tried, the more life came back into my arm. I could feel my brain remapping every nerve, muscle, and my motor control, fibre circuits going back to normal as I regained control of my elbow and fingers.

My right side was so weak that Del had to help me get dressed. Bit by bit, strength came back into the right half of my body, to the point I was able to get up and walk downstairs to the ambulance waiting for me.

To my surprise, two of my sisters, Jean, Nicky, and my brother Tony, were downstairs in the hallway. "When did you lot get here?" I asked, delighted and surprised to see them.

"You gave us a fright. We thought you had a stroke," Tony replied.

"I'm OK now. Just got to pop to the hospital to find out what's wrong. See you in a bit," I said, quite calm and confident.

I felt fine but had to lie down in the ambulance. The paramedic checked my blood pressure, which was still very high. All that was happening did not seem real. I wanted to believe it was just a storm in a teacup and there would be a simple explanation when I was checked over in the hospital. In the back of my mind, though, was this question: what if something is seriously wrong with me?

While the ambulance made its way to the hospital, lying on my back and staring into space, I began to reflect on my life over the last two years. In January 2008, I could not have felt healthier. I was jogging early every morning at 5.30 a.m. five days a week, running for the bus for work each day, eating mainly fruit, vegetables, chicken, fish, drinking water, no fizzy drinks, no butter, sugar or sweets. Losing weight and feeling very sharp and agile, I felt good, especially out in the morning fresh air. On certain days, I would head towards the public footpath, off the main road, up the embankment. You would never believe the amount of farmland and playing fields hidden behind a hedgerow. One minute you are on a main road with lots of heavy, noisy vehicles speeding up and down, with people standing at the bus stop or walking into town, and the next you're looking as far as the eyes can see over pleasant playing fields, farmland, fields with horses roaming around. The busy main road noise can't be heard as it is replaced with the pleasant sound of nature, birds whistling, trees rustling in the gentle breeze, the sound of my own feet pounding through the field and my heavy breathing.

After completing a 3 km fun run in April 2009, I felt so good I could have run it twice. I didn't even break a sweat. My fitness regime went out the window though, after a bad toothache, which lasted two months. There was no more jogging or eating healthily. Some months later I tried the fun run circuit to get back into jogging mode again; I did not even get a quarter of the way around the circuit. I had to admit defeat, walking back sweating, hands on my hips, mouth open wide, trying to catch my breath. I felt awful.

I tried picking up where I left off in the October. It lasted two weeks, and I stopped after passing blood when going to the bathroom one day. This freaked me out. I had all the check-ups at the hospital. There was no high blood pressure, no bladder or kidney infections. I got the all-clear and felt good again.

Del also had a health scare, so we both had a wake-up call.

We decided to review our work–life balance to reduce our relentless, stressful, weekly chores of managing four children, four after-school activities, our day jobs, and also our business ventures and weekend activities consisting of more children's activities: netball, football, music and dance lessons. To top it all, there was looking after my mother and father every Sunday. *That's heavy going*, I thought. But we continued with our stressful lifestyle.

In October 2009, I took part in a free health-screening programme. I was so upset with the results; what an insult to be told I needed to see my doctor to get a second opinion because my blood pressure was high. I have never had high blood pressure in my life, so I ignored the advice.

In November 2009, Del went for a ten-day break in Jamaica with her sister. She needed a break.

My mother became ill that same month, and my brothers and sisters and I spent the whole of Christmas coming and going from the hospital until she passed away on the 8th of January 2010. "What a coincidence," I said to myself. I was still reflecting: *this time last year it was my mum in hospital, now I am going in.*

2010 was a horrible year. In the recession, we lost out financially twice with companies going into liquidation. I can also never forget Friday the 13th of August when I wrote off my car by wrapping it around a lamppost. I don't know how I lost control, but miraculously I walked away from the wreckage. I broke Del's new nine-feet hallway mirror she was so proud of. Everything seemed to be going wrong. When would it end?

Well, it did not stop there. I smashed up my other brother Alex's sports car. I also noticed my right arm was weak when playing the sax. Runs and riffs I could previously play without thinking I could not do any more. I put it down to lack of practice. Come to think of it, I could not pick up my right foot fully when walking. It was very noticeable, especially when on holiday in Spain, when I was almost dragging it along. Again, I put it down to ill-fitting sandals. It was upsetting tripping up the stairs at work; yes, my right foot kept catching on the odd step every now and then, no matter how much I tried to prevent it. It never occurred to me that the whole of my right side was slowly shutting down.

Lastly, did I have a blackout, or was it that I was so tired I fell into a very, very deep sleep? I recall, at my daughter's netball tournament, I popped back to the chalet with Ryan and Miles, my two young sons, for a quick drink. We had a ten-minute break before my daughter Amaris's final netball match. I watched impatiently for them to finish their drink, and the next thing I remember was the horn going off for the end of the match as I slowly woke up. Forty-five minutes had gone, but it felt like I was only there for five minutes. Where were the boys? I could not account for the time. *I must have been very tired*, was my excuse. I discreetly got in with the crowd as though I was there all the time. I stopped reflecting when the ambulance came to a stop.

We arrived at the hospital and I was admitted by the paramedic team. I was wheeled into a temporary cubicle until a bed was available.

Chapter Two
The Manor Hospital

I sat in the cubicle with Del, waiting forever to be seen by a doctor. I was uncomfortable and getting restless. The cubicle had two hard plastic chairs to one side and an examination bed on the other side, with levers and pedals for various adjustments. We both sat facing the entrance that was obscured by a drawn white curtain which prevented us from looking into the corridor. There was a lot of hustle and bustle, with doctors, nurses, paramedics and cleaners walking up and down, each dealing with all kinds of issues. It was so busy the whole noise blurred into one hazy, distant sound as we focused on the stillness of the cubicle with its blank walls.

My mind was void. I had no idea what had happened to me. Was it just a dream?

After a long time, a doctor emerged with a big smile, "Mr Lewis, could you sit on this bed and remove your shoes? Just make yourself comfortable, please. I need to perform some checks."

I did not answer, just did as I was asked. I took my shoes, scarf, hat, and coat off. He held my head up and shone a light into my eyes and told me to look into the distance. He did not say anything. He then used his hammer to check the reflexes in my knees and feet.

"Could you lie on the bed now, Mr Lewis? I'm going to push down on your ankle. I want you to resist and push upwards. I'll do this with each leg in turn."

I followed his instructions.

"Now, I want you to bend your knee. I'm going to push against your leg into the bent knee position. I want you to resist and push against what I'm doing. I'll do this with each leg."

I noticed that my right leg was much weaker than my left leg. He still did not give anything away. Del and I were bemused by these checks; we did not know what possible relevance they had to what I recently experienced.

"Now, can you sit up and outstretch your arms towards me? I'm going to push them up. I want you to resist and push them down, then we'll swap around. I'll push them down and you up," he requested.

"OK," I replied.

This was done. Again, my right arm was much weaker than my left. As I am left-handed, I did not think any more on the matter.

"Lastly, could you outstretch your arms with your palms facing upwards, then reverse them with your palms facing downwards? Also, could you close your eyes while doing so?" he said, indicating with the tone of his voice he was coming to the end of the checks.

"No problem," I replied.

When I opened my eyes with my arms still fully outstretched, I observed that my right arm had dropped. I perceived it to be at the same height as my left hand. I could not tell it had dropped. Also, my right hand had turned inwards with my thumb, index finger and middle finger slightly curled. It's not something I was aware of. The doctor did not say any more or give an explanation of his findings; he said thank you and disappeared behind the curtain. Del and I looked at each other and pulled facial expressions to agree we didn't know what was going on.

Another doctor came in after a long time. We had been in this cubicle well over four hours by then and we were tired and hungry. He came with the results of an MRI scan I had taken months before, but never had the results. It was a scan from my neck downwards after I had convinced the doctors back then that the car crash I was involved in trapped a nerve in my neck, affecting my right arm. According to Del, I had an answer for everything, which was not always correct.

"We have your results, Mr Lewis, but there are no signs of any abnormality. The results are fine," said the doctor, looking at the scanned images.

"What happens now?" I asked.

"We'll have to book you in for further checks. You'll need to have another scan to see what is going on."

A nurse came along and took two swabs, one from my nose the other from my groin. She then clipped a wristband to my left arm with my hospital number on it. Shortly after, a tall man all in dark blue entered the cubicle with a wheelchair and called out my name.

"Yes?" I responded.

"I have come to take you over to have a CT scan[1] done," said the man. I got up and sat on the wheelchair. He checked my hospital number on my wristband then wheeled me through a series of long corridors following the green line marked out in the middle of the floor. We eventually went through some double doors and up a little ramp into a waiting area. There, in front of me, was the door leading into a room where the scanning machine resided. To the left of me was a set of lockers. I had to remove my phones, keys and coat and put them in a locker before going in for the scan. The man introduced me to the female assistant who would take me through when it was time for me to go in. He said, "I'll come back to fetch you when you're done," then left.

---

[1] See the glossary of terms.

"Mr Lewis?" I turned around in the direction of the female voice. "Could you follow me please," said the assistant. I got up and followed her into the room. I stood by the door as she explained the procedure.

"This procedure will take roughly twenty minutes. We are going to do a scan of your brain to see what's going on." She used layman's terms to make sure I understood.

"You will lie on this bed, which will take you partially inside the unit. You will hear strange noises and sounds. Don't worry, that is quite normal. It's part of the procedure. Then you will be taken out again, and that's all there is to it," she said reassuringly.

"If at any time you feel uncomfortable and you want to get out, just press this emergency button. Are you OK with this?"

"I'm fine with that," I said, taking it in my stride. I just wanted to know what was going on inside my head.

The scanning machine was in two sections. The first part looked like a conveyor belt bed. It could be elevated higher or lower to suit the person who would lie flat on his or her back. It was covered with a disposable blue, moisture-absorbent, hygienic sheet before each patient used it. Once a patient is on it, the conveyor belt bed is elevated to allow the patient to be transported into the second section of the scanning machine.

The second section is a large cylindrical unit. The conveyor belt bed moves the patient head first into the cylindrical unit until half their body had disappeared inside. It is very claustrophobic inside. Patients may become traumatised, so there is an emergency button to press in case they panic. It shuts down the machine and gets them out quickly.

"Could you get yourself ready then, Mr Lewis, by taking your slippers off and lying on the bed, please?" she said politely, pointing to the bed.

"Sure," I replied.

She disappeared into a side room where all the controls were.

I did what I was told, lying on my back looking up at the surgical lights in the ceiling. The machine elevated me up to alignment with the entry point of the cylindrical unit, then pulled me inside. I did not realise how confined the space was. Suddenly, I was gripped by a feeling of fear that I couldn't get out, the more I looked around and felt my helplessness. In trying to move, anything could happen, I thought. I had to close my eyes and remind myself of the panic button. I tried to think of something else other than where I was; this calmed me down, and I began to relax.

The machine started up like a washing machine going through a spin cycle. I remained extremely still and did not attempt to open my eyes. I imagined this cylindrical unit rotating around me. There were a series of sounds – beeps and mechanical noises – all around me. I kept perfectly still. I did not feel any changes in me, sickness or anything like that. I just endured the process, encouraging myself that everything would be all right.

At last the machine started to shut down. The spin cycle was coming to an end, and I was slowly pulled out of the unit. I waited until the assistant came back into the room before moving. I opened my eyes.

She walked back in and said, "You can get up now, Mr Lewis. It's all completed. If you wait outside, the chap that brought you across will take you back. The doctor will have your results the next time he sees you."

"Thank you," I replied.

I went outside the room, collected my things from the locker and sat back in the wheelchair, waiting to be pushed back to the cubicle Del was waiting outside. She came with me. Eventually, I was collected and taken back to the cubicle.

For the third time, another doctor came this time. It was a female, and she went through the whole checking process of the previous doctor. No one was telling us anything and Del had become annoyed and was getting more and more frustrated, but she kept quiet and waited patiently. The female doctor completed her checks, then left. She gave us the assurance that someone would come back with more information.

I can't remember which doctor was the main one, as I had seen so many. However, one of the previous ones came again.

"Well, Mr Lewis, before we make any conclusions, we need to take another scan. The first scan, if you like, is like a black-and-white image of your brain. It doesn't show much detail; it produces a cross-sectional view of your brain. The second scan will be an MRI [2] scan. This shows more detail but requires a special dye to be injected into your bloodstream to aid this process. We have scheduled another scan. OK, Mr Lewis?"

"I guess I'll have to be."

I began to wonder how long I would be in hospital.

A lady pushing a wheelchair arrived to collect me for the MRI scan. I went through the same procedure as before but the difference was a nurse applying a cannula into the back of my left hand and injecting a dye into my bloodstream while I was lying on the conveyor belt bed. A cold and strange feeling came all over my body as the dye spread into my veins. I started to fall asleep after twenty-five minutes. This process took much longer. After the scan, I was once again back in the cubicle. I had been there since about 1.30 p.m. and it was about 9 p.m. and we were still in the cubicle.

About two hours later the doctor assigned to me entered the ward and came over with some paperwork in his hand. "I would just like to go through some more checks with you."

By this time, Del's patience had run out.

"But this is the third time you've done this. What actually is going on? We haven't been told anything. We've been here since 1.30 now. We don't know if he has to stay in hospital, or what the problem is. What's his situation?" she demanded.

---

[2] See the glossary of terms.

Del already had in her mind that I had experienced a mini stroke and was expecting some kind of confirmation on this. Her own father went through a very similar experience some years before he passed away, so it was something familiar to her. I think she had already prepared herself on what to do to help me recover.

"We have your results back from your scan. We can see a dark shadow over the left frontal lobe of your cranium." He paused for my response.

"What does that mean?" I questioned.

"You have a meningioma. It's about the size of a golf ball."

"What's a meningioma?" I enquired.

"It's a brain tumour on the left side, which is why you had the problems on your right side. The left half of your brain controls your right side and vice versa," he replied.

Del went very quiet.

"A brain tumour the size of a golf ball," I repeated, looking at Del. "That's not that big. Well, at least I know what caused the stroke, the weak arm and trailing leg," I said reassuringly.

I turned my attention back to the doctor and asked, "What happens now?"

"Well, we don't have the expertise here so you will have to be admitted to the QE.[3] They specialise in neurological injuries and illnesses. We will arrange a transfer for you. First, we

---

[3] Queen Elizabeth Hospital.

need to find you a bed until the transfer is arranged. Is your wife OK?" he said, changing the subject.

I quickly looked at Del. Her whole body was shaking uncontrollably and her teeth were chattering. I had seen that before – she was in shock. Whenever Del is in shock, that is what happens. I got out of my seat and walked towards her and held her close.

"It's all right. What you've just told us has put her in shock. She'll be OK in a few minutes," I replied. He waited a while before leaving the cubicle.

Later on, a bed was found for me in a ward where the men were predominantly old with very bad respiratory conditions. They seemed near death; they were very ill indeed. It was very disconcerting. As ill as I was, I did not see myself that way. I was still in disbelief and had not yet come to terms with my own situation. The men had bad coughs with audible heavy wheezing. As the man next to me coughed with a sustained exhaling, I wondered if his lungs were going to collapse before he would breathe in again. Then the next patient would sound off with an even deeper, louder cough, as if a call-and-response round of wheezing was in concert. It was very upsetting to see and hear. It made me worry a little, thinking that would eventually happen to me. I reassured myself I would only be there for a very short time, then would be going home.

Jim, the man next to me, pressed the button to call for assistance. When the nurse came, she said, "What's the matter, Jim?"

Hardly getting his words out, he spluttered, "I can't breathe."

She checked the monitor and noticed his oxygen levels were low. She fetched a nebuliser[4] and put him on that for about half an hour, which eventually stabilised his breathing.

I started to put my clothes away and make myself comfortable in my new surroundings. There was a bed with clean blue and white linen, which was adjustable to whatever position I found most comfortable; there was a hand controller with all the buttons to adjust height, make it upright or flat and knees bent or flat. Next to the left side of the bed was a tall portable cupboard in two sections. The bottom half had a front-opening door large enough to hold my small sports bag. The top section was smaller and had two opening doors at the side facing the bed. I put my phones in there. On top was nothing, and cartons of juice or fruit could go there. On the right side of the bed was a comfy chair and a height-adjustable table tray on wheels. The wheels would slide under the bed so I could eat my meals in bed. Each morning a nurse would replace a jug of water and a cup on the tray. All around the bed was a curtain rail with a floor-to-ceiling curtain draped back. When privacy was required, it was fully drawn all the way around.

At about 2 a.m., Jim's breathlessness had started up again. He pressed the attendance button for a nurse. He sounded worse than the last time. He had to take a number of breaths

---

[4] A breathing machine asthma sufferers use to open up their airways so they can breathe.

before he could get out each word, and I began to feel anxious for him. To me, he sounded like he could go any time.

The nurse came along. "Nurse! I'm dying!" Jim said in a pitiful voice.

Rolling her eyes, the nurse said very cheerfully, "No you're not, Jim. Your chest is playing up again? Come on, I'll sort you out." She calmed him down and put him on the nebuliser unit.

Jim was distraught and fed up with his condition. He kept taking his mask off and shouting down the ward, "Why don't you just let me die! I can't take any more! Nurse! NURSE!"

It took some time for the staff to calm him down. His breathing was very heavy; I could seldom get to sleep because of the noise. I was worried about him. It seemed like he would not make it through the night. I eventually fell asleep but awoke in the early hours of the morning to the nurses doing their routine checks and administering medication. I looked over at Jim and there was no noise – he was sleeping like a baby.

The next day at breakfast, Jim was awake and in good spirits. He was certainly a different person compared to the early hours. I pondered, *is that what happens to you when you feel all hope is gone?* I certainly did not feel that way. I did not think it was healthy for me to be in that ward.

Later that evening, I was moved to another ward. It would be another day before I was moved to the QE. That evening it dawned on me: "A tumour the size of a golf ball," I whispered as the realisation hit me. "That IS big. Wow!"

It was my fourth day in the Manor Hospital, a Tuesday. The seriousness and implications of my illness were far from my understanding. As far as I was concerned, this was just a process to go through. Once the experts at the QE had seen to me, did what they needed to do, I could go home and get on with my life. I just did not know when I would get to the QE.

I pondered on what was going on at work. It was my week to be on call. There were three of us in our section, and one of my colleagues was on holiday. I dreaded the thought that I dropped the others in a mess by being in hospital. I sent many text messages and made phone calls from my hospital bed to my friends, work colleagues and family, even though I was not supposed to. They all must have thought this was out of character for me; I'm normally very quiet, slow to catch on with the office banter and generally more the serious type. For me to be pulling a prank would be unheard of. When I texted them about my illness in a very casual way, that I had a stroke and was diagnosed with a brain tumour, they were bemused. I sounded normal and certainly gave no indication I was seriously ill. I recall having a phone conversation with someone at work I would not normally speak to, but he called asking how I was. He must have heard the rumours, thought it bizarre, and wanted to hear for himself.

The news had hit my community about my illness. I can only imagine it came as a big shock. There were nurses I knew fairly well working in the hospital, and they all came to see me when they got a chance. A few friends were there as soon as they heard. All this attention was very humbling; all this fuss for me.

My mind was empty. Everything was going over my head. I knew Del and our children were fine, so I left them in God's hands. I was in the middle of sorting out a business venture that had seen hard times. There were final notices from our creditors, deadlines from the various banks we had loans from, and I was expecting a call any minute from one of them. *The other directors will need to pick up where I left off*, I thought.

Every Sunday was the day I would look after my dad. The carers would have washed him and given him breakfast by the time I got there. I shaved and dressed him, ready for church, then took him back home. I would prepare him dinner, check his blood sugar levels and administer his insulin, and have a little chat before heading home again. Every other Tuesday was my sleepover night; my brothers, sisters and I – all thirteen of us – would take it turn to look after Dad, only I could not do it anymore. Someone else would need to fill in for me.

How were my boys going to get to football training and drum lessons? My older two children were doing GCSEs and A levels, and I hope it wouldn't create a distraction for them. It looked like Del would have to manage it alone.

All those thoughts rushed through my head, making my mind spin and my heartbeat race, but then an inner peace came over me and gave me reassurance that everything was going to be all right.

***

"Your blood pressure has come down, Mr Lewis," said the nurse after strapping my arm and finger to the portable monitor and noting the readings in my medical notes. This reassured me even more. I began to relax a little; I felt fine and was in good spirits.

"We have found you a bed at the QE, but it won't be available until later this evening," said the nurse as she approached my bed.

It was late. It must have been after 11 p.m. I had gone to bed but was woken up by two paramedics. They introduced themselves and told me they'd come to take me to the QE.

"Do you need assistance to get on the trolley bed?" they asked.

"No, it's OK, I can manage."

Half asleep, I cleared the cabinet of all my belongings. When I got on the paramedic bed, they put my belongings on top. I had my dressing gown with the blankets from the bed wrapped around me.

The snow had settled. I thought that it looked like we were going to have a white Christmas that year. Another four days and it would be Christmas. The journey was slow and bumpy. Again, I thought about how funny the situation was. At that time the previous year, my siblings and I were driving backwards and forwards in the snow and cold to New Cross Hospital, where my mum was seriously ill. We were told she might not make it, and she passed away a week into the new year. A year later, there I was in a very similar situation. I couldn't imagine how it must have been for my family – first it was Mum, then me.

We eventually got to the QE, where it was very quiet and still. I was wheeled out of the ambulance and taken to the Lower Ground B Ward.

The ward was awkward and confusing to get to. Coming through a side entrance, there was a set of automatic slide doors, dimly lit, and there was an unmanned reception area with a couple of magazine racks loaded with medical literature. Like a moth, we followed the light source. I was wheeled through the slide doors, and the area opened up into a brightly lit corridor. There was no sign of life, and it was very quiet and peaceful.

The corridor was long. We spilled out onto a walkway somewhere in the middle. Along its length on one side was a restaurant and, a short distance along, a newsagent's. There were various doors to offices, all painted white. Between those doors, the walls were decorated with large educational posters displaying information about neurology, brain tumours, and the like. On the other side were art déco-style windows looking out at other sections of the building.

We turned left down the corridor towards the direction of the ward. Near the end, we turned right into another long stretch of a corridor. Immediately to our right was a lift.

"Lower Ground B is on the next floor up," said the paramedic.

"That's very confusing, considering the fact we are already on the ground floor. How can lower ground be one floor above?" remarked his colleague.

We entered the lift and pressed the button for the floor above. When the doors opened, we turned right towards the entrance of the Lower Ground B Ward.

The ward sister was waiting for me. "Hello Mr Lewis," she said, "you're in bay five."

All the patients had gone to bed, so it was very quiet. Not all were sleeping though and, as I passed by the other bays, some were watching movies or reading books.

The paramedics wheeled me into bay five, where there was a bed prepared for me.

Chapter Three
The Queen Elizabeth Hospital

The Bay

I quietly put my belongings on the armchair next to the bed. On the left side of the bed was the storage cupboard. I put my phones in the side cubicle.

It was an old building, but it was warm and comfortable. I made the bed comfortable and climbed in, using the controls to lift the top half of the bed so I could sit up. Over my head was a green and white swing arm. At the end of it was a touch-screen monitor with a built-in phone attached to the side. For a fee I could watch movies, make phone calls, surf the web or just watch TV. It seemed all very expensive considering it was just normal TV. I pushed the swing arm to one side so the touch-screen monitor would face the wall.

Once I had settled down, I looked around the bay. There were four beds in each bay, two against the side walls, each separated by a wooden portable cupboard and an armchair on either side of a bed. At the far end of the bay by my bed were two windows in the back wall, looking out over other sections of the hospital. In the distance you could see a snow-covered road, like a white blanket. Between those windows was a sink. Above it was a wall mirror and also a hygienic hand wash dispenser with a green bottle inserted. On the floor on each side of the sink were two bins with foot pedals: one for clinical waste and the other for general consumer waste. Each bed had flat screens on an extended, retractable swing arm, which allowed you to watch TV, listen to music or surf the web in private.

Things have changed so much since the last time I remembered visiting my mum in hospital. Then, there was one TV for a whole bay and there were always disputes about which channel it should be on, whether it should it be on at all or if it was too loud. Now we had our own individual screens with headphones, so there was no disruption to other patients who wanted peace and quiet. At the opposite end of the bay was the walkway, which linked all the bays. No need for doors to enter each bay – they were all open-plan. The sidewalls, shower rooms, or toilets separated each bay.

Nurses and doctors would scuttle up and down to demanding patients or for routine check-ups. We all had a nurse button on an extended lead, which was plugged into a socket on the wall by each bed. We simply pressed it when we needed help and it would give off a beep every few seconds until a nurse came to assist. I found out later, if you pulled the lead out of the wall, there would be a different sound, which meant there was an emergency. Doctors and nurses would come running, ready to deal with the emergency.

Those in My Bay

The lights were off in the bay. Only the lights along the walkway were on, which dimly lit up the area. There were four men in my bay. One night, two of them were sleeping but the other, a young soldier called Denny who was injured in Afghanistan, was opposite me with his face illuminated by the reflections of the screen as he watched a movie with his headphones on. He had a white bandage wrapped around his head. You could tell part of his skull was missing, as it was sunken. It was surreal and a bit of a culture shock – could someone be alive and function with half their skull missing? I noticed he had a wheelchair by the side of his bed and he did not move his left arm much, if at all. The whole of the left side of his body was paralysed. He used his right arm to move his left leg around and regularly called the nurse for assistance. He did not speak much. He seemed so young. He had many military visitors, apart from his mum and dad, who visited him very often, considering they were from London and we were in Birmingham. I later met his mum and nan, and we got on very well.

He was a paratrooper; HRH The Prince of Wales was the head of his regiment. Whenever soldiers got injured, they would be brought to the QE for treatment. It was at the cutting edge of technology for major breakthroughs, clever inventions and human robotics. The hospital got a lot of media coverage and publicity. The QE specialised in neurology. It's second to none in the UK, so if you wanted the best treatment, you went there. I was in the best place.

In the cubicle next to Denny was Sid. He was a retired accountant, but still kept himself active. He was a chairman of some social club and managed their books. He was also the sole carer for his wife, who suffered with Alzheimer's. He was a very nice man, tall and thin with silver hair. The glasses he wore had small, rounded lenses. Sid was a very emotional person. He constantly worried about his wife, that no one was looking after her while he was in hospital. He wanted to move to a hospital closer to home. He asked to be transferred to Good Hope but was disheartened when he was told the best hospital for his injuries was in Shrewsbury. He had suffered a nasty fall in his garden and lost all feeling in his arms and legs. He could not walk or move his hands properly. Each day he got better, but he had to lie on his back for six weeks without moving. He had already been like that for a week. When he first came in, he could not move at all, having damaged his spine when he fell.

When his wife visited him, he burst into tears at the sight of her, which was a very touching scene. When he had composed himself, he gave her instructions and advice on what to do on sorting out their affairs. Even in his condition, he was still active.

Next to me was a very thin, bearded man called Hussein. He was all twisted in the bed and very poorly. He was never awake, all the time I was in that bay. He never ate his food and barely responded to the nurses. The curtains were often drawn around him. I never really got to know anything about him. At one point, the nurses had to wake him to make sure he was not unconscious.

That night, I turned over onto my right side and eventually fell asleep. It was my first night in the QE. I consciously slept on my right side, slightly curled. Whenever I would turn in the middle of the night onto my left side, somehow I would wake up and turn back to my right. The memory of the stroke made me very uncomfortable and uneasy sleeping in that position.

In the early hours of the morning, I gently woke up to a series of clinical sounds. I heard subtle footsteps along with the noise of turning plastic wheels, and occasionally there would be a clunking, metallic sound. There would be a pause, then whispers from a nurse and a quiet response from the patient. The pulling apart of a Velcro strip would break the silence. As I looked up, a nurse wrapped the Velcro strip around Sid's arm. The motor from the blood pressure monitor made a whirring sound, then stopped. It was a portable contraption on wheels. The nurses recorded their findings in the patients' log book, then moved to the next patient.

Eventually, she came to me. I did not know her name, but she appeared very childlike. It felt quite strange to be looked after by someone who seemed so young; I'm used to looking after myself. It felt awkward. I'm sure she could not have been much older than my daughter.

"Mr Lewis, you've got a scan in the morning. Your consultant, Mr Saleem, will come to see you before you go. Is that all right?" said the nurse.

"That's fine," I replied. When she moved to the next patient, I got up to go to the toilet. I realised I could not walk properly, no matter how hard I tried. I just could not lift my leg high enough, and my right arm automatically went into a hook position across my chest. Consciously, I would put it down by my side but, as soon as I stopped thinking about it, it would go back.

As I headed for the toilets, I took note of my surroundings so I would know which way to get back to the right ward.

The Old QE

The QE is a very old building, but a new section was being built. Most of the staff were being moved across as each phase of development was complete. The neurological wards were the last to go as the specialist equipment was still in that block, so all patients with head or brain injuries were in the surrounding wards. There were the odd few with back problems.

Later on that morning, I underwent two scans: a normal CT scan and then an MRI[5] scan. Each time, I was wheeled back and forth from my hospital bed.

––––––––––––––––––––––––

[5] Magnetic Resonance Imaging.

A good while later, my assigned doctor emerged onto the ward with more results. The nurses would reassure me, "The doctor will be coming to see you soon." This seemed to be a coded way of saying, "You might see him, but I don't know when."

The doctor said, "We have the results back from the MRI lab." He showed me a set of images of my brain. I could roughly make out what the dark area on the left side of my brain looked like. Imagine a small baseball cap, the size of a slightly oversized action figure, upside down. One part of the dome part was sunk all the way down, about one inch into my brain on the top left side, with the flap sunken, facing forwards in line with my left eye.

"You have a meningioma about the size of a golf ball. For it to be that size, you must have had this for a while. It's been there at least three years," he said.

"What is a meningioma?"

"A brain tumour. It is in the meninges. That's a layer that separates your brain from your skull," he replied, trying to explain in layman's terms. I did not respond. "If you could choose a type of tumour to have, this is the best one. You're very lucky. This is not attached to your brain, but it is indented into your brain. We will need to excise it."

All the information did not mean anything to me, and just seemed to float over my head.

He concluded, "That would be the reason you experienced all those symptoms on the right half of your body. The left side of your brain controls the right half of your body and vice versa."

He then moved to the next patient in the bay.

Logically, I began to think, *Oh! That's the reason I'm walking funny, my right arm is weak and why I could not play the fast brass parts on my sax*. I reassured myself I had an explanation for my symptoms. Peace came over me, even though I had no idea what I was about to face.

The Ward at Night

I got used to the sounds at night; it was quite peaceful and calming for me. Most people were bored, worried, in pain, confused, or wanted to go home. I was at peace and had no worries, apart from sleeping on my left side. Luckily, I did not come across anyone who was screaming, frantic or irrational. I supposed my mind and body had a chance to switch off, making the most of the break from my constant, day-to-day stressful lifestyle. I did not have to think about work, the band, my dad, the business venture, or my family. I just believed they were well and everything would be all right. In any case, worrying would not have helped. I was not in any position to do anything. I trusted in God, so I slept well and was getting rest.

There were times I was restless and needed something to occupy my mind, so I would listen to the different sounds throughout the night. They intrigued me, especially the sound of the nurses walking up and down, their footsteps rebounding off the concrete floor. I did form my opinions;

those who were the hard workers tended to wear flat shoes. They moved swiftly up and down the wards. The sounds were like soft, short, quick, scuttling movements, not harsh or abrasive. I would test myself to see if I knew who was coming up the ward, and most times I got it right. Those who were senior tended to wear stilettos. They seldom smiled and did not have much rapport with the patients, but rather talk at you, about you, around you, but hardly to you. It gave me the impression that, once you're in a hospital bed, the conclusion is you're sick, therefore you've lost your ability to understand. It came across as patronising. Not all the nurses treated you that way.

I got used to the daily routine until I knew it like clockwork. Firstly, the night shift nurses would come around the wards about 8 p.m., routinely checking all the patients' blood pressures, heartbeat, and oxygen levels. Then the locked medical trolley would be wheeled in with a laptop resting to one side, but only qualified nurses could administer the medication. They had the key to open the trolley. They would check your wristband against your details on the laptop to make sure you got the right medication. The consultants would do a morning round about 6 a.m., however, in reality I found the consultants for the other patients would come around, but my consultant I only saw when I was due to go into theatre.

At that point, patients would begin to wake up. The still quietness of the night would go through a transition into a hustle and bustle as the early workers, cleaners, and ancillary staff came on shift. The tea and water woman or man would change all our water jugs and cups for clean ones. We were always encouraged to drink plenty of water to prevent dehydration, or to have a hot drink. It would not be long before the air would be filled with the smell of food, and at 7 a.m. we would have breakfast.

The cleaners and bed changers were next to appear. I made sure I was first in the shower so I did not have to wait in a queue and, by the time I got back to my bed, it was freshly made.

There were no visits before midday. The first one was between 2 p.m. and 4 p.m., after lunch, and the last one would be 6.30-8 p.m., after supper. I knew what time of the day it was by the timing of the meals. I would be looking for the next meal almost straight after the last one. I would be feeling very hungry, which was unusual for me, but I guess it may also have been the effect of the steroid medication. I became accustomed to the routine. I certainly could see how quickly one can become institutionalised.

It's not nice to see patients with no visitors. It's as though they've been abandoned, even though I know there may be many justifiable reasons behind the scenes. It was not practical for Del to visit me during every visiting time. The journey from where we lived to the QE was long and expensive, but she did it twice every day, so I told her only to come in the afternoon. I did feel anxious and abandoned during visiting hours when Del did not come. I would be watching the clock, minute by minute. When she finally came with the children, I would be at ease.

After the visitors had gone, the tea and water trolley would return, and so would the medical trolley. The doctors would normally do an evening round, especially if you were going into theatre the next day. After that, some of the patients would read a book, listen to music, watch a movie, surf the web or just go to bed.

I learned very quickly to be a friend to the nurses – that would go some way to me being well looked after. I could categorise the different types of nurses: the good, the informative, the vindictive, the matter-of-fact, get-over-it type and those who were appalled by the very people they were trained to look after. Not to mention the cheeky, friendly, and caring ones. When certain nurses were on duty, I could relax and rest assured it would be a good day. But, when the not-so-nice ones were on, I would keep quiet, especially if I did not feel too good. In any case, I tried to keep myself as independent as possible.

"Mr Lewis," I heard my name being called. I opened my eyes and Mr Saleem, my consultant, was standing at the side of my bed with a nurse. I had fallen asleep. "Mr Lewis," he repeated.

"Yes," I replied.

"How are you today?" he asked as he inspected my head.

"Fine, thank you."

"Well, Irvine. Can I call you Irvine?" he asked, looking at my medical notes.

"Yeah, that's OK," I replied as I sat up and made myself more comfortable in the bed.

He started to explain my condition, then the course of action.

"Irvine, you have a grade one-type benign tumour. You are very lucky; these types are the better ones to operate on. They are not attached to the brain and don't normally reoccur once removed. Now, you're on a course of steroids to reduce the swelling, thus reducing the risk of seizures or a stroke. You will need to take along with this a stomach-lining tablet; the steroid on its own can cause stomach ulcers. We will also prescribe paracetamol, co-codamol and an anti-seizure drug."

"What about the operation? What happens then?" I asked.

"Firstly, we will do a blood test to make sure you're fit for surgery. You will have a general anaesthetic and we will cut away a bone flap from your skull to excise the tumour, then put the bone flap back with staples."

"How long will this all take?" I asked, as though I was talking about someone else and not me. I was totally detached from my very serious illness and the full implications of surgery.

"The operation will take roughly three to four hours. We do these operations all the time. They are fairly routine."

I fell silent after that.

"The anaesthetist will come to see you and explain in more detail the procedure. Is that all right, Irvine?" In concluding, he was moving to the next patient.

"Yes, that's fine," I replied. My mind was empty. I was not emotional, worried, stressed, fearful, or sad. There was this stillness in my mind. I was not thinking of anything. I really did not know what to think or how to act with the information I was just given. I was sure, in the future, the reality would hit me, but there was nothing.

I got myself a hospital pair of pyjamas and settled down in my bed with a book, a biography of Nelson Mandela, and started to read. Hussein's curtain and Ben's were drawn for privacy.

The night was calm and quiet. The landscape looked dismal and lifeless. Birmingham had not experienced sub-zero temperatures like that for many years. The ground was covered with a thick blanket of snow that had hardened to ice. Inside my bay, it was warm and comfortable.

After sitting up in bed reading some more about Nelson Mandela, my mind drifted away from the book as I looked up and gazed into the distance, not looking at anything in particular. My mind homed in on the Lord. I have always felt close to God. Often, I would share my thoughts, fears, hurt, pain and joy in simple prayers or meditation. I started to reflect on the conversation I had with my consultant, knowing I had embarked upon a journey unwillingly and I couldn't walk away from; I didn't have any control over where it was leading me or how things would turn out. I leaned upon my faith in God that everything would be all right. I said a simple prayer to the Lord, but it was more like I was telling Him what I wanted rather than asking. I guess it was more a cry of reliance, knowing that my situation would be hopeless without God. I said, "Lord, if I must go through with this, then supply only the best surgeons, doctors and nurses to operate; those who are well rested and not tired. I must be the first one in theatre for that day. Let all those involved with me be excellent at their job and genuinely care for people, not stressed, weary or sad, but very positive and uplifting. In your name, Jesus, I ask. Thank you, Lord."

I did not get the answer straight away, but I knew He would answer. Over the years, the relationship I had with the Lord was invaluable to me: I knew Him and He knew me; I could not talk that way to Him otherwise. I had confidence He would answer.

When I could not read any more, I pressed the button on the bed hand control to lower my head a little, then pressed another to raise my knees up slightly, turning myself to the right to a comfortable spot. I fell asleep.

The Sea of Prayers

As I slept, I recall in a vision my eyes slowly opening. I gradually became aware of my surroundings, suspended high up in the atmosphere, looking down at a church steeple. The atmosphere had no colour; it was all transparent. The church appeared like a pencil line drawing of a faint white colour sketched out in the atmosphere. Little bubbles at first floated out of the steeple, like a child blowing bubbles through a wand. There was a constant flow that increased in volume. They just kept churning out of the church; they were definitely drifting slowly up towards me.

I noticed that there was no definition to the atmosphere. I could not see a horizon, just the vast space I was suspended in. Bubbles started to appear from everywhere, not just from churches, but also from other locations. I understood it to be from people, friends, family, towns, cities and countries. I watched in amazement. As these bubbles drew nearer to me, there were millions of them. They bunched up together like when foam is created when washing-up liquid is stirred vigorously in water. As I focused on a few bubbles, they were also transparent. Inside each one was my name. These were individual prayers for me! There were so many compacted together, they formed a great sea. You could no longer see bubbles, just a great sea of prayers flowing together like a transparent sea. Each ripple and wave were only highlighted like an artist's pencil sketch.

This sea of prayers rose up underneath me and elevated me even higher in the atmosphere. I was flat on my back, floating on this sea with my head tilted forward, looking at my feet. My arms and legs were spread out like a starfish. Again, I was defined as a pencil sketch. Other than tilting my head, I could not do anything except float on this sea.

The atmosphere was engulfed with this sea of prayers, so much so it caused a shift in the heavens. There was no way it could go unnoticed. There was an expectation something was going to happen any minute. I can't explain it, but whenever I have a supernatural experience with God, I instantly know who it is. By the time my eyes have closed then reopened in a split second, He's there, and I have no time to prepare.

I felt a presence come down towards me. I knew those prayers called Him and got His attention. He drew near to investigate. I could feel an air of authority, a commanding, loving yet non-judgemental atmosphere. There was no fear in me. I instantly knew it was the Lord. I became overwhelmed that He came to see me. I could feel His presence as He drew near to the left of me. I tried to turn to see, but I could not turn. The Lord would not allow me to. I could not see Him but I knew His voice. The excitement for me was so great I became like a child; my heart was aching with joy, full of peace and contentment. This was a once-in-a-lifetime kind of experience. I said excitedly, "Lord, you value me that much. You got all these people to pray for me?"

"Yes," He replied. "I value you that much, and so do all these people."

My face lit up with happiness, and joy filled my heart. I was humbled, honoured, and absolutely overwhelmed that the Lord valued me. He came down to see me and all these people were praying for me. It was more than a cloud-nine experience. My illness paled into insignificance compared with this encounter. It's an experience I will never forget.

The Lord then said authoritatively, "It is already done!" Just those few simple words rang out in my ears, in my mind, and most definitely in my spirit. I knew I was healed. That was the foundation of my confidence and positivity, regardless of how dire my situation became. I drew my strength from those words.

Throughout my time in hospital, I would have flashbacks of that visitation. It meant so much to me. It was at a time when I had experienced many setbacks to my aspirations and dreams. These setbacks had left me feeling unappreciated, misunderstood, taken for granted, but the most painful heartache of all was feeling unvalued. I felt like a ghost – there, but not seen. This made me more determined to fulfil my dream, as nothing else seemed to fill me with life other than attempting to fulfil the purpose of why I am here. After all, when my body became crippled with the stroke, it was the reminder of my unfulfilled dream that unleashed a hidden strength of faith to rebuke the hideous sickness that invaded my body. I had a second chance. It was not my career, my family or friends, but knowing I had entered life and was about to leave without fulfilling why I was there in the first place. I was going to live and bring the dream and vision to pass before I died. Knowing my assignment was not yet complete made me even more determined.

The visitation was not my first encounter. I have had others before, but that one was different. It was the beginning of a series of spiritual sessions I received that challenged me in every way. It challenged my logical reasoning, faith, understanding, trust, and obedience.

Looking back, there was no fear in me, but had it not been for those supernatural experiences that manifested in the real world, I would have dismissed them all as bad dreams and having a far-fetched imagination. Some dreams had actually happened, while others were prophetic and futuristic.

After this, I started having dreams of people who were a part of my life. When those dreams occurred, I knew they were praying for me. In one case, I woke up about 1.45 in the morning. To my astonishment, stood by the side of my bed, not in body but in spirit, was my brother Godfrey. He was in prayer, then he disappeared. I quickly got my phone and texted Del to tell him thank you for praying for me and that I heard him praying at 1.45 that morning.

Del did what I asked, and when Godfrey got the text, he was also astonished, because that was the exact time he was praying for me.

I had so many messages from so many people telling me how they were praying for me. They were from people who knew me, knew of me, or had been acquainted with me at some point in my forty-five years of existence. I could not comprehend why so many people, some I barely knew, cared about me. The visitation was real.

The Green Disclaimer

On December the 30th, 2010, Del sat by my bedside when the anaesthetist came in with the green disclaimer forms for me to sign. I hadn't eaten anything that evening as I was once again nil-by-mouth for the umpteenth time in preparation to go into theatre first thing in the morning, New Year's Eve.

"Right, Mr Lewis, all you need to do now is sign these forms and put the gown on in the morning before you go into theatre," said the anaesthetist.

"Hmmhh, OK," Del and I said as we began to read the disclaimer.

I recall reading: "you could have a seizure, stroke or even die". This information just went over my head. Del would not look at me. I said while slowly looking up, "Well, I leave it in your hands, Lord. You said it's already done."

"Amen to that," said Del.

"I know it all seems a bit daunting, Mr Lewis. Reading all that sounds worse than it really is. Obviously, we have to point out the worst-case scenario so you are fully aware of what can happen while you are in surgery, for legal reasons." The anaesthetist was trying to reassure us, as she could see the worried look on Del's face. It did not make Del feel any better. As for me, I did not have a choice, so I just signed the papers.

The next morning, the anaesthetist came to collect me, all gowned up. I had to put on the theatre gown, then have another cannula inserted into the back of my left hand. My bed was wheeled into a middle passageway between the theatre and the corridor. Before I went in, Del and I said our goodbyes and waved at each other. I have no idea what she was thinking or feeling. All I remembered at that point was when my daughter, as a child, broke her arm. She was in the same position I was in. I held her hand until the anaesthetic kicked in and put her to sleep. She disappeared behind the doors into surgery, where the doctors were going to set her broken arm. I never saw her until a few hours later. During that time, I felt helpless and could do nothing for her; she was in the hands of the surgical team. I had to wait patiently, hope and pray that all would be all right. Del was now in that position with me.

While in that room, a possible point of no return, the anaesthetist put all these EEG patches on various parts of my body and said, "Before you go into theatre, we are going to put you to sleep. I'll slowly inject the general anaesthetic into the cannula. You will feel a little pain, then a funny feeling and, within a few seconds, you will be asleep."

I said, "Well, here goes."

She started pumping the fluid into my arm. I remember saying, "This feels funny" and then I don't remember anything else.

While I was under the general anaesthetic, the surgeon made an incision in my scalp and used a special drill to bore a hole into my skull.

The hole was about 1 inch in diameter. The consultant told me that the best type of tumour to have if you have one is a benign one which is what I had, a meningioma.

This was not in my brain but in the layer of the meninges, so it was separate from my brain, but it was pushing down into the left side of my brain, causing the right side of my body to slowly shut down.

This affected my speech, memory, visual memory, physical coordination and movement. My responses were slow in conversations.

The surgeon with precision removed the tumour, taking care not to damage any healthy tissue. After the operation, the bone flap was put back in place with staples also with a drain to remove any excess fluid.

I must have been awake with my eyes open, but not aware of where I was and what was going on. All I remember is Del and my sisters, Jean and Marie, sat there talking to me. I was talking back to them, and probably talking too much. I can't remember what we were talking about, but I came around very quickly. It was about ten minutes later before it registered with me what I was actually saying to my visitors. I felt great, no pain, no odd feelings. I felt a million dollars. I was tempted to get up, run, and jump. I was certainly on a high – it must have been all the medication I was on.

When all my visitors had gone, I noticed that time was going too slow, or so I thought. I sat in bed watching the clock periodically, waiting for the new year to be ushered in. It felt like I had been waiting for three weeks, but it was only mid-afternoon. When I looked at the clock, only fifteen minutes had passed. I recall being very impatient and thinking a lot. I was not tired, but sat in bed very, very still, not moving an inch but watching the nurses as they passed in front of my eyes, where I was focused. They sometimes stopped and waved in front of my eyes or asked if I was OK. I would respond with a smile or answer that I was OK. I must have been like that for hours, but it felt like forever.

Chapter Four
Visitors

***

Family, Friends and Notable Visitors

During my time in and out of hospital, I had a few notable visitors – not that any were more important than the other, but some were more significant to me. If I did not believe the words from God that I was valued, he was proving it to me with all the attention I was receiving.

Until then, before I had the stroke, there were times I felt like a ghost. It was as if I was there, but nobody saw me, whether at work, home or church. I did not feel valued; I must admit, this made me feel very hollow. I subconsciously put all my energies into looking after my mum and dad and playing in the band because that is where I felt most appreciated. Apart from that, I tried to make sure I was a good father and husband. I did my duties: cook, clean, fix this, fix that, take the boys to football training, football matches and music lessons. I did not want Del to be lumbered with too much to do, so I made sure I did my part.

The emptiness and insignificance I was feeling from those around me made me more determined to be closer to God. I did not know exactly how I was going to do it, but I did spend a lot of time meditating, sometimes praying, but mostly talking to God as my friend. His presence gave me a warm, peaceful feeling that really comforted me.

I was merely existing – but trying to find a better meaning for my life. I decided that was my lot in life, that it didn't feel fair, but I was going to do the best I could and be the best I could be. I did feel that I was taken for granted sometimes. But I was determined. I would make myself happy and value me – not for anyone else, but for me.

My expectations were not high of people wanting to know how I was doing. I did not set my heart on any great expectations from visitors. I tried to remain as independent and occupied as I could. I did not want to rely on anyone but God, not even Del. Since the visitation, I was in my own world with God; nothing else mattered to me. I did not even think too much about getting out of hospital. In fact, I did not think at all, but took each day moment by moment. Having visitors was nice, but I did not set my heart on it. But I was humbled and flabbergasted by the amount of attention my illness had drawn.

Paratrooper Denny

Denny was a soldier injured in the course of duty in Afghanistan, was very young and almost childlike in his looks. I tried not to stare too much, but I just could not get over how he was alive with half his skull missing. He was quiet and spoke softly until his soldier friends came to visit from his regiment, when he would become more himself, talkative, jovial and lively. Denny had a constant stream of military officials of various ranks visiting him, along with the military nurses.

He had come a long way in recovering from his injuries. When he was in Afghanistan at a station post, a stray bullet from a sniper ricocheted off the floor and up the back of his helmet, then exploded, taking out the right half of his skull. No one thought he would make it through, but he made a remarkable recovery. He had the best treatment available from the QE. His left side was totally paralysed and he could not move his left leg or arm, from what I can remember. He was recovering gradually, and was able to feel his big toe, with some involuntary movement occurring. His mum and Nan were very friendly. The family was not local, so the military put them up in a hotel near the hospital so they could be close. At some point, when he was well enough, he would be transferred to a military rehabilitation centre nearer his home. Each time they visited, they brought a lively atmosphere with them, which broke up the silence in the bay.

It was clear that Denny was well taken care of, with future plans for his rehabilitation.

As each day went by, I did not think anything about what was going to happen to me. I did not really know, either; I just followed the flow of each day: wake up, go through my checks, shower, eat, a visit from a doctor or not, eat, a visit from Del or not, more checks, read a book or sleep, eat, another visit from Del and the children, then sleep. This was pretty much the cycle.

HRH Prince Charles and Prime Minister David Cameron

It was Christmas weekend, and I had lost count of the many times I had been told "you're going into surgery soon" or "you're nil-by-mouth today", but nothing seemed to happen.

As I sat up in bed reading a book, two military nurses came in to see Denny. They made sure he was clean and tidy and made a fuss of him. They tidied the area all around him, and any half-filled sanitisers were replaced with full, unused ones. Come to think of it, even the military nurses had brand new green and white uniforms on. The floor was cleaned, and any and everything that was out of place was put in order. It was all very unusual; there seemed to be some big expectation. Sharon, a bubbly nurse, came into the bay and, in passing, said, "We've got royalty coming." I did not think any more about it and continued reading my book.

The hive of activity began to increase, and more senior military figures kept coming in and out around Denny. His parents then walked into the bay.

"Hi Irvine," said his mum and Nan. "We've got royalty coming today!" said his mum, excitedly.

"What do you mean, 'royalty'?" I asked, but we were distracted by more military officials coming in, so I never got an answer to my question. I just assumed they meant the top man in the QE was coming down. Two military nurses stood on either side of Denny's bed in a very official and orderly manner. It was a bizarre scene indeed, with their arms in front, backs straight, looking dead ahead and very military like.

Besides Denny and I, the other two patients were oblivious to what was going on. Hussein was asleep, while Sid was preoccupied with his condition and could not sit up because of his injuries.

All of a sudden, like a whirlwind, about four tall men in suits came in swiftly and stood in very strategic positions around the bay, so I sat up and took notice. I could hear talking coming from down the corridor that got louder as it came near to the bay. The next minute, in walked HRH Prince Charles and David Cameron, the then prime minister. It took me aback: walking swiftly towards Denny were two of the most important people in the country. They were standing in front of me, because Denny's bed was opposite mine. Denny's family stood up and formally greeted them both. It was all too surreal.

Prince Charles began the rapport with Denny, discussing his situation, then David Cameron. There were smiles and laughter. I sat in amazement, still coming to terms with these top men in front of me. The visit could not have been more than ten minutes.

"I hope you get well soon," were the words from both VIPs as they concluded their conversation. As their bodyguards walked in front of them towards the corridor, first HRH Prince Charles turned towards me and looked me in the eye, and waved his right hand as he repeated the same words he told Denny: "I hope you get well soon."

I stumbled with my words, as I did not know what to say or how I should respond to royalty. I'm sure I said thank you.

Next, David Cameron did the same, giving a right-hand wave as he repeated the same words: "I hope you get well soon."

I said thank you, still a bit stunned that they spoke to me. They both disappeared back the way they came, with the entourage following them. I tried to take a picture before they left the bay, but struggled to steady my phone with my weakened right arm to press the button. All I managed to capture was a disappointing blur.

I noticed that in my bay the only people they spoke to were Denny and I. Hussein was curled up in his bed and they did not seem to notice Sid.

"He's very nice, Prince Charles, isn't he? But David Cameron, he did not answer my question!" said Denny's mum. We had a little chitchat as the realisation of who had been in our company soaked into our minds. After that, we turned to doing our own thing. I sent a text to Del and my colleagues at work, letting them know I had just seen the prime minister and Prince Charles. I kept in touch with them even though I was in a hospital bed.

It was quite bizarre, but after the Lord told me He valued me, I became a joyful soul. No one would believe I had a brain tumour; I was very joyful and at peace, in contrast to those I was in hospital with. They seemed down in spirit or confused and struggling to come to terms with their conditions.

There were signs on the walls saying not to use your mobile phones, but the cost and the inconvenience of using the public phones encouraged me to use my mobile even more. It was not costing me any extra, and I did not need to leave my bed and, besides, it was a text, not a phone call.

After sending the text messages, I sat back on my bed and smiled and had a personal talk with the Lord. *Lord, you're joking with me*, I thought, and smiled. *I heard you when you told me that you valued me, but I can't believe you've got the two top people in the country to come into my bay and tell me to get well soon.* I continued smiling. I knew the Lord was letting me know what He told me in the visitation. *What a way to endorse it*, I thought.

If that was not enough, as the tradition goes when you're ill, you get a lot of visits from friends and family. I had that, but there were some notable ones. I did spend Christmas at home, and all my brothers, sister, Del's brother and sisters came to visit me. I was truly spoiled. I became the centre of attention and made the most of it. Then I was back in my bed in the QE.

Karen and May

While Del sat with me, Karen and her friend May popped in to visit. I had not seen Karen for three to four years, and May,

I did not know. They brought me gifts, and when they began to talk, it blew my mind. Without me saying a word, Karen told me the time, day and on what side I had my stroke. She is a prayer intercessor who prays on behalf of others and sometimes takes on their burdens on their behalf. She told me her husband nearly took her to the hospital because he thought she was having a stroke, and she had to convince him that she was fine and was carrying it for someone else. She had stroke-like symptoms and had to take time off work. She called her prayer team, and they prayed. When they prayed, the Lord told her she was carrying the burden for me. She then contacted Del, who confirmed to her that I was ill and in hospital. During the visit Karen had encouraged me even more and gave me a revelation from the Lord.

May began to speak to me. She seemed a little reserved and unsure. She asked me what was significant about the number seven. I could not answer the question because I did not know what she meant. She too had an experience: a severe headache for seven days where she had to take time off work. Her husband became worried about her too. She was new to taking on someone else's burden through intercessory prayers, so it was a new experience for her. She knew who it was but had never met me. At the church she attended, her pastor counselled her and told her she was carrying the burden for someone else. He described me to a T, having never met me and I had never met him. He also was interceding in prayer for me and with May, sent a prayer shawl, which I kept on my shoulder constantly throughout my time in hospital until it mysteriously went missing on the only day I put it down before having a shower. She, along with

Karen, had encouraged me and told me I would be fine and would recover.

There was a significance about the number seven. The Lord told May that the person she was carrying the burden for would have a number seven over his head. She was disappointed when she saw me that she could not see anything around and about me that she could link to the number seven, so for her, it did not make any sense. I did not know what to make of it, and searched through my mind to see if I could find anything to give her an answer. That night my spirit was troubled, because I wanted to know what it all meant, and could not seem to find any resolve.

It was not until I was in intensive care after having the tumour removed that it all made sense. During visiting hours, someone pointed out I had a number seven over my head: I was in bed number seven, so it looked like it was over my head, like May mentioned. This was a kind of confirmation for both of us; the encouragement I received from her, her pastor, and Karen were now endorsed. However, it was not until 2017 that the real meaning was revealed to me, and the Lord enlightened me that the number seven meant seven years. I would be ill for that amount of time. When I got this revelation, I excitedly got in touch with May to let her know that the seven meant seven years of sickness. 2017 was my seventh year since the tumour, and it was also the year I came off NHS support, started jogging regularly after a cruciate ligament knee reconstruction operation and the time I got my driving licence back after being seizure free for over a year. It was the beginning of me getting my life back.

During my time of illness, the Lord was constantly giving me confirmation after confirmation of the value He placed on me and also his reassurance of his plans for me. I was more than overwhelmed and felt very blessed.

Del was constantly telling me of the messages she was receiving from people who were praying and those who had a message for us, who were enquiring about my welfare.

I could not take the boys to football, but I was overwhelmed by what Del told me. Some of the parents from the boys' football teams made sure our boys were picked up from home and dropped off to training on Saturdays and their football matches on Sundays. Del did not have to do much; they kept in touch and looked after my family while I was ill. This was one of the most treasured acts of love in demonstration I have ever experienced, and there were two very special families who looked after my boys. Words are not enough to express our appreciation for their kindness, hospitality, and charity. They gave up their time and money willingly to see that our boys were taken care of, so we did not have to worry. This lasted for about three years! I still can't get over it. I class them as our earth angels.

Bishop Brooks

Bishop Brooks is a straight-talking man who doesn't mince his words, but he is very discerning and direct. His passion has always been for marriage and family values. I was so shocked when I saw him walk up the ward corridor while I was sitting up in bed. Once again, I thought, a bishop coming to see me?

"God bless you Brother Irvine. How are you?"

"Bishop, good to see you. I'm doing very well, thank you."

"I have just come to let you know you will be fully healed," he said directly.

"I know, and believe it," I agreed.

"How's the family?"

"They're all doing fine under the circumstances," I replied. There was a little silence, so I began to tell the bishop how I heard the Lord call me as clear as him talking to me when I was on holiday in Spain, saying, "Why don't you have a family prayer in the morning?" So I did.

Bishop Brooks said to me, "You know, when the Lord gives you a directive like that, it's not a one-off, but a continual thing." Since then we've tried to keep the prayer going but not managed to do it every morning.

It was a quick visit. He said bye and went on his way up the corridor.

I sat back and thought about the visitors. I could not make any sense of so many visitors, and notable ones I would least expect. I thought, *this must be a sign of things to come.*

Phone Messages

As Del sat by the side of my bed, she pulled out her mobile phone.

"Irv, Vinney and Sandy send their love. They are praying for you. In fact, the whole church is praying," she said, reading from her phone.

"That's nice," I replied.

"Mr and Mrs Johns phoned for you. You're on their prayer list at their church," Del continued. "Also, your cousin, she sent a prayer message out on Facebook. Mrs Bell, Mrs Grissett, Mr Bentley and Mrs Drake have been asking how you're doing."

There were so many people concerned about me that it did make me feel special.

I could not help but wonder how Del was coping within herself. I would ask, but she would always reply with a smile, "I'm OK. Don't worry about me; it's you I'm more concerned about."

She drove a thirty-mile round trip practically every day to see me, sometimes twice, after taking the children to school, doing a day's work, picking the children up, feeding them, then going back to the hospital. I know if it was me, I would've been worn out, but she's a hard worker.

I had my phone with me all the time I was in hospital. I kept it on silent so no one knew when I received calls. I also discreetly made calls. My phone would frequently vibrate with the many text messages I received. I started scrolling through the message from my sister-in-law:

"Hi Irv, sending blessings to u as u prepare for your Op, later today. Will be thinking of u. xx Jen ps-I'll give you a rain check on this one for not coming to London, but don't do it again! As we say in JA.. Walk good now 23/12/2010"

When I read it, I started to laugh, as I thought back to when we would go to London and she would have a long list of things for me to do. I would take my toolkit to fix, repair, install, configure, etc. You name it, I would do it. We were due to go down to see her, but life had other plans for me. I did not have the operation that day – it was cancelled.

I had another text message from Dave, an old friend from my teens:

"Hi Irvin Dave H, here heard the news from Jenny. My prayers are with you. Jehovah Rapha is with you at this time. God bless you sir,"

I had a message from the bandleader:

"Hi Ervin, our prayers are with you and your family. God bless you and keep you all."

I also had a message from Karen, who had come to see me with May, her friend. She texted my sister with this message:

"Amen! He shall recover. Please tell him from me, I have petitioned for full recovery so he can play his sax for the glory of God. He is a worshipper. "

There were so many messages, it made me feel warm inside. The concern and good intentions overwhelmed me. I don't think I have ever experienced receiving so much love before; the whole experience broke the scales.

Bernard and La jira Praise

Bernard was the bandleader of a praise and worship band I was a member of until it broke up. We supported each other during a time when we were both pursuing our dreams in the music sphere.

I remember praying and asking God to put me in contact with people who would help me musically, and Bernard was one of those people. The very next day, he called me and asked if I wanted to be involved with a music project he was managing. Until that point, I never knew him. He got my number from someone I played for about three years earlier and it went from there.

We found that we were both very passionate about worship. The band performed at various functions and was very lively. I recall doing various recordings in 2009 just after the band split up due to key members moving on. I stayed and supported Bernard even though I was playing with another band. About a month before I was seriously ill, I had a call to do some recording. I distinctly remember struggling to play at speed with my right hand. I just could not play my parts in time. I put it down to tiredness and it being late. We agreed to redo it at a later date. I got a call to finish off the re-recording but, by then, I was in a hospital bed waiting for surgery. He came to visit, prayed and encouraged me. He, among many, believed I would recover and continue to play music.

He said to me, "I'll give you a call when you're back on your feet and we can continue where we left off."

He continued to keep a check on my progress and, three years on, I got a call that he had finished the album. He kept the original recordings of the songs I did and wanted me to play at the album launch. That was a challenge. I had to relearn my own solos, knowing that my right hand was slower but, somehow, I had to find a way of playing them at the same level as I did before. I managed to find alternative ways of playing certain notes that would lessen the need for a speedy response from my right hand, with most of the work done with my left hand. All this was a boost for me. Bernard kept a video diary, which has been so interesting. Although it is about the band and its journey, inadvertently it also covers a little of my journey before being diagnosed, just after surgery, but still in recovery and three years on.

Chapter Five
All the Prayers

My Dad and Siblings' Prayers

My whole family was devastated when they heard about my illness — Del, the children, my brothers, sisters, nieces and nephews — Del had to console so many family members. I don't think Del could even deal with her own grief while reassuring others. My in-laws were in shock. They gave my family so much support. All the support we've received is invaluable to me. They were all relieved when I recovered quickly and came home. It was short-lived, as I ended up back in hospital with a brain infection. They did not know what to do – they were lost and bewildered until Grace, a prayer warrior and intercessor, picked up something in the spiritual realm about me and called my family and sternly told them I needed covering and that they needed to pray for me.

As a result, my brothers and sisters started a weekly prayer meeting on my behalf. They would meet on a Monday each week and pray for me to be healed. My dad was a man of prayer; he could pray for hours. Once he got started, it would be difficult to stop him. He was always praying. This has rubbed off on my siblings and me. Wherever they were, they would make their way to the family home to pray, and it was a very powerful, encouraging, and a hopeful time. Their faith was strengthened to believe that I would not die.

When I came out of hospital the first time, coincidentally, one year to the day since my mother passed away, they all gathered at my house to celebrate me being back and also to remember our mum. I was out of hospital for two weeks before the stroke-like symptoms returned. I felt hollow inside and unstable on my feet. My right hand would shake uncontrollably, like someone suffering with Parkinson's. I had no strength on my right side. I would get repeated, sharp pains in my head exactly in the spot where the tube was protruding from my head when I was in hospital. Needless to say, I was rushed back into the QE eventually, but that's another story. They tagged a nil-by-mouth sign on me before I left the ambulance, and I would have gone straight into theatre that same day if there was space.

My whole family, friends and work colleagues were mortified and in disbelief. They did not think I could possibly make it through this time. My family, along with many others, continued to pray. An email sent around my workplace that I saw many months later indicated I might not return to work. They did not think I could possibly recover from a brain infection. "Our thoughts are with his family," were the concluding remarks. But I made it through.

The support I have had from my family can't be measured. They bought every health supplement and aid device. You name it, they got it for me. They cooked our meals, cleaned our house, supported Del, checked that we were OK. All our in-laws were equally supportive.

My work colleagues were the same. I would get personal, encouraging messages on my wage slip from payroll each month while I was on sick leave and the occasional phone call from my department.

Dreams of Friends and Church Prayers

While I was in hospital, I would have dreams and see people or acquaintances I knew randomly. It turns out each time I had a dream about them was when they were praying for me. I have mentioned the time with my brother, but there were others. When I saw them in my dreams or a vision, I knew they were praying. I could feel their prayers. When I was able to see them, I could tell them and confirm that they had prayed because of what I saw.

My Local Church

In all the years I have been attending this church, it's the first time I was able to objectively see, feel and experience the love shown towards me and my family through their prayers, visits, gifts, well-wishing and constant support. It is a comfort and support network for my family and me. It's always been said, let others see the Jesus (love) in you. I can honestly say I have experienced it through my illness. They constantly prayed for me and my family. There was a time when all my veins had shut down so they could not put in an intravenous drip, which was needed to kill off the infection. They immediately stopped and prayed and, within minutes, a doctor came and found a vein (I'll explain in more detail later).

Mother Gordon and Jean Gordon

Jean Gordon and Mother Gordon are two people I am very grateful to for their constant prayers and encouragement. They constantly prayed for me to be healed.

I'll never forget the dream Mother Gordon had about me. She is a very tiny lady, but don't let her small frame deceive you: she was no pushover and very sharp and abrupt, but very loving. Jean is a prayer warrior who is constantly praying. Her home is like a prayer centre. People were constantly meeting there to pray and intercede on behalf of others in need. Mother Gordon said to me one day after I had come out of hospital, "Irvine! I got a dream about you, you know. You were climbing up this ladder up to heaven. As you got near the top, you fell off and banged your head! But you know what? You're going to climb that ladder again and reach the top. What are you waiting for? Get back up that ladder!" she said very sharply, slapping my arm at the same time, but lovingly in her own way.

Mother Clarke, Thompson and Brown

Sister Thompson and Sister Brown are very silent workers in the church. Not only were they constantly praying for me, but they would be checking on Del and the family and making sure they were OK, very discreetly.

Mother Clarke was like my second mum, a very important figure in my life and those who were regularly at fasting service. She was a part of the fasting group at my local church. Without fail, every Thursday morning, she would be knocking at God's door in prayer for me to be healed. I was destined to be healed because so many people prayed.

The Bethel Organisation

I was on the prayer list of all the church congregation. This humbled me, and I was more than grateful. I'll never forget. I lost count of the number of pastors, elders, ministers and friends who were constantly enquiring, visiting and checking on my family, making sure we were all OK.

Lorna and Richard would send me text messages or make phone calls to encourage me. Vince and Sandra constantly called, sent text messages, and really looked after us. I saw the power of unity and togetherness from an organisation and the impact it has. When people are united for a cause, there is nothing that cannot be achieved. My healing and recovery is proof, and an example of united prayer.

Chapter Six

One to One:
Out-of-Body Experiences

I realise the spiritual encounters I had experienced are known as out-of-body experiences and that other people have had them, too. The realisation kicks in that there is life after death; death is just a separation of the flesh from the spirit. The flesh dies, but the spirit and the consciousness lives on in the eternal world. It would seem that earth and everything in it is real and heaven and hell is a dream or an imagination but, after death, the phrase is turned on its head – earth is the dream and heaven and hell is the eternal reality. The human spirit is eternal and lives on.

The physical me is just a house I live in given to me at birth when I entered this earthly reality so I could exist and live in it, experiencing what life has to throw at me: a mixture of good and evil to test how I respond and what I choose to do with my valuable free will.

One to One

My time in hospital somehow became a school of learning certain life principles and some spiritual enlightenment. The things I learned came from acquaintances, family members, old friends, new ones, my spirit going into the supernatural realm with some important lessons from the Lord. The thing is, some of them we already know: forgiveness and how important that is, telling loved ones you love them, not just telling them but also through some good deed or form of action, settling differences with people, making sacrifices of your time and resources for the benefit of others without looking for something in return. Most of all, valuing people, not just in words but active, real compassion that cares for every human being. One thing is for certain: when you are in a life-or-death situation, wealth, money and popularity can't help you. They don't mean anything. Most likely, in that situation, you'd think, "When I get out of here, I'm going to …". Your perspective on life will change if you get out of that situation.

In my experience, I often get visions, dreams and conversations with the Lord. I admit it was difficult for me to believe, and I had to write them down, then read them back to myself to see if they made any sense. Some of these far-fetched visions or dreams would manifest in the real world, so if I had any doubt, the proof or evidence would be there. In fact, it's all been a unique experience that I feel quite privileged to be able to write them. I also found that I began to see deeper into biblical scriptures I had been reading for years and grasped something more from them I never saw before.

One night while in my hospital bed, I became aware I was in a special place. I was physically in the hospital but my spirit was in the heavenly's. It was a vast space with no evidence of height, depth or breadth. I could not relate it to any landscape or horizon. I was suspended in the atmosphere. There was nothing to see. It was pure. I was not floating; I was just there, suspended. I knew I was high up but could not say how high. It was an exclusive and personal space. There were no distractions there, only truth. It was very peaceful, with no fear, but spiritually warm and restful. I recognised a certain presence I had experienced before when I had the vision of the sea of prayers. I was in the presence of the Lord Jesus. Just the two of us. The feeling I had inside was beautiful. It was definitely a utopia, and I wanted it to last forever. My soul was constantly satisfied and refreshed. I did not want it to end because the feeling was pure. The Lord's focus was on me and nobody else, and my focus was on the Lord and nothing else – it was totally exclusive.

He could see straight through me because I was transparent. It was my spirit. I could not hide my thoughts or my feelings. I was totally exposed and naked. I tried my best to think the best thoughts as I became anxious that, any minute, my impure mind would betray me with some bad thoughts and I would not be able to stay in his presence, and would be kicked out. His overwhelming presence of power, authority, truth, righteousness, clear discernment of me, His royalty and, most of all, love, made me squirm with unworthiness. I was totally transparent, and he knew everything about me. He could see my thoughts floating through the atmosphere, coming towards me before they reached my mind, so he knew what I was thinking before I did.

I tried to be on my best behaviour but, being in His presence, I could not be anything else but who I was really, the real me. As individuals, we can mask our true feelings and responses to questions and things said to the point people would never perceive, whether we are for or against what we've responded to. To go further sometimes, we could be laughing inside or be very angry or thinking a whole lot of things in response to what we've just witnessed, but no one would know, because it's kept inside.

Not so with the Lord. Exactly how you thought it or said it to yourself or would respond with arms in the air, facial expression and sarcasm, etc. is exactly how you would respond in the Lord's presence. You could not hide or cover up your true self. You would be exactly who you really are. That said, He accepted me as I am. He never judged me, just loved me. It was a parent–child or father–son relationship. In this atmosphere, age did not matter. I was a child. He was very patient with me as he began to teach me spiritual things I would object to, in true character, with disbelief, slight sarcasm and childishness. The Lord would just stop and wait for my understanding to catch up. When it did, I would feel so foolish for not seeing it the first time around. I would repent, agree with His words, then He would move on to the next lesson.

I learned very quickly to agree with the Lord, trusting that He was right even when I did not understand. "Two can't walk unless they agree" is a snippet from an old proverb, and I found it to be true for me to walk with the Lord. I had to agree with Him, otherwise we would never move from the standpoint we were at. He would never abandon me there, but expected me to learn before we moved on. His love for me, His son, was very apparent. He made it known how much I was valued and cared deeply for me. It was as though He was pleased with me, but I could not get my head around why He chose me? In any case, I was more than pleased He chose me. I knew I was highly favoured and privileged. This was definitely a once-in-a-lifetime experience. There is nothing I could compare it to. The Lord came to see me on a one-to-one, in person, and you can't get better than that. He taught me some things I found difficult to accept. He had to open up my understanding so I could receive what He was teaching me.

Time did not exist in that dimension. I was out of time, or it stood still. For how long, I could not tell. All I know is that I was with the Lord, and it felt like a very long time. In fact, time was not relevant. It had no meaning there. All that mattered was the Lord and me. It could have been ten minutes or three hours, I don't know. All I know are the things He taught me.

One of the first things the Lord said to me was, "Irvine, anything that is cursed of God, you have a right to curse it and send wherever you choose. Whatsoever you bless shall be blessed."

I replied, "OK."

He started to enlighten me about Genesis chapter six. He said, "Irvine, it was the fallen rebellious angels that corrupted the earth, man and beast. They took the daughters of men and produced half-angelic, half-human creatures. These beings are superhuman with the gifting of man and angels. Equally, the rebellious angels also corrupted the animals, producing half-angelic/animal creatures again with the abilities of both parents. Sadly, man has corrupted himself likewise with animals."

I responded with "Oh" as I tried to take it in.

"Irvine, because these creatures came about through rebellion, they were born cursed. They don't know me and have no concept of love. They only have pure hatred for God and anything good. They inherit the same fate as their rebellious parents. They were not meant to be, so there is no place for them other than that prepared for the rebellious and cursed of God. Because these creatures are part-human or part-angelic, they are a spirit but have nowhere to go when they die until the appointed time. They have inherited their father's inheritance: eternal damnation. They try to rob those that are in the land of the living of their opportunity, to my inheritance that I have provided for all men, if they choose it. You know these creatures as devils, demons, sprites, ghouls, or evil spirits. There are many other names they are called by. They seek to possess living beings, mainly humans, where they squat. All these corrupted beings have abilities and/or a gift depending on the inheritance of their parents. The gift is not what you think – it is more like an inheritance that is passed on to those they possess: sickness, disease, soothsaying, wickedness, dark heart, addictions, obsessions, depression and many other traits."

The Lord continued, "These creatures make up the kingdom of darkness, which is a space between earth and hell. They are united with Lucifer along with some people against the kingdom of light, that which is seated in the heavenly realms. The kingdom of light is united with God and His angels against the kingdom of darkness. The prayer from the dark kingdom is opposite to 'Thy kingdom (God's) come on earth as it is in heaven'. Theirs is, 'Thy kingdom (Lucifer's) come on earth as it is in hell', but be not afraid – you have authority over all the kingdom of darkness."

He reminded me, "Anything that is cursed of God, you have a right to also curse it and send wherever."

The Lord continued, "The kingdom of light is pure love, my love. You will find warmth, peace, and rest. This is where souls who are set free dwell and their eyes are enlightened to the truth in my presence. It is a place far above principalities and powers. The kingdom of darkness is pure evil – there is fear, torment and no rest. This is where souls are bound in spiritual chains by their strongman, who has taken them captive, and their minds are darkened so they can't perceive the truth, my truth. Their lives are miserable and they are helpless. Many are oblivious on either side of the fact that they that are free don't realise they dwell in heavenly places. Likewise, those that are bound don't realise they are held captive in the kingdom of darkness bound by a strongman whose intention is to keep them there until they die, keeping them from ever knowing who they really are, manipulating them to use their gift for bad or else preventing them from using them at all. There are those who also know and are aware of this and choose which side they want to be on."

I sat back and started thinking about what I remembered reading in Genesis 6, how the earth was corrupt and full of evil, so the Lord gave it a time limit when he would remove man off the earth except for eight souls – Noah and his family. It took me a while to take this information in. It kept going through my mind.

I recall the Lord putting things before me. I can't remember much detail about the things other than I would ask, "Can I curse it?" If the Lord said yes, I would curse it and send it to hell and watch it go backwards into the ground. If I said "dry up and die" it would wither before me. If the Lord said not to curse, I would not say anything, and it would pass by.

After this lesson from the Lord, my spirit was very alert and, often, seeing something going on somewhere in the spirit realm, I would discern the evil and curse it and send it back to hell and it would happen. In fact, my words became very sharp and anything I said came to pass. I distinctly remember one case where I saw something evil attached to something that was good. My spirit was ready to deal with evil, but my attention was caught by the part that was good. I was moved with mercy and I had to zip my mouth so that I could not say anything; I had to just focus on the good part until it passed by. If I had opened my mouth to deal with the evil, it would also cause the thing that was good to die, which I could not allow to happen. I set my heart on the Lord to check if this was the right decision, and it was.

The Kingdom of Darkness

During a time in intensive care one evening, about 8 p.m., I began to fall in and out of sleep, but it was very weird. I would doze off, but then, suddenly, I would be startled awake from going into a deep sleep by hearing a sound or a noise that would become distorted and warped. When this happened, I experienced strange things. In every case, I could feel my spirit being summoned on some kind of mission. These sounds were like calls and, each time I got a call, my spirit would leave my body and jump into the kingdom of darkness, similar to jumping over the side of a boat, only it was jumping over the right side of my bed. I always knew what to do without knowing if that made any sense. It was as if my reasoning faculties were switched off while my spirit did what it was summoned to do. It was always going into the kingdom of darkness, binding up a strongman and setting the soul free that the strongman had bound in chains. I did not necessarily know who I had set free, but every one of the strongmen – or should I say spirits – were subject to me. They had to do what I told them when I bound them; they were bound and could do nothing. I would then break the chains of the bound and tell them they were free to go. I would then jump out of that place and back into my body in reverse order. The call would come from the Lord. It happened so often that night; I was tormented from sleeping. All I wanted to do was sleep, but I was not allowed to. As soon as I was startled by a sound, if it did not warp or become distorted and was a normal sound, I would doze back off into sleep. But, shortly after, I would hear that warped sound and would say to myself, "Not again." After a while, I would complain to the Lord and say, "Lord, not again. I'm tired. Just let me sleep for a while."

In my experience, the kingdom of darkness was just pitch-black. You could not see anything; there was no floor. It had depth and width, felt low and base; you could not tell how deep or low you were. I had no idea, positional-wise, where I was, but each time I went in, I knew exactly where to go and how to come out. When I confronted a strongman, I could not see them but I knew what to do. I could not see the bound, but knew they were there. It was full of fear and very dangerous. You could not go to this place unless you were sent, otherwise you would never return. Many people have their souls bound there even though their physical presence is still in the land of the living.

This would manifest through sickness, disease, demon possession, wickedness, strange lifestyles, mental issues and evil practices. Once in that place, you would need deliverance. The deeper you went, the more evil it was and the stronger the strongmen.

Some weeks after, I thought about those experiences. In a dream one night, I saw myself from a distance going into the kingdom of darkness. I could not see my face, only myself from the back. I thought, *How come I was not afraid? Why did not anything happen to me?*

As I was thinking those thoughts, I saw myself being rotated, and I drew nearer to myself. As I rotated, I saw my face: it was a bright golden glow shining like a bright light. This golden glow was the authority of the word of God written all over my face. I could not see the creatures in this dimension, but they could see me coming and knew what I was going to do. My understanding was enlightened. I heard in my mind, in my own words as a conclusion, "It's not so much me they were afraid of but the word of God that was written on my face that gave me the authority to do what I had to do."

When I realised this, I thought, *I'm going to study the word of God more because it is key to tearing down spiritual strongholds.*

My Encounter with Cronus

In the early hours of the morning, I found myself in a strange but familiar place: the blackness of the floorless place, the kingdom of darkness. I was standing directly in front of a huge, demonic spirit. I was not afraid as it was subject to me. The difference was this spirit had like black on the outside, but was luminous on the inside. I only knew this when I had to disarm it. It was in the shape of a gigantic man.

My task was to disarm it by speaking authoritative words while I cut it in four places, across the joints where the arms connected to the shoulder and the legs connected to its body. With each cut, it exposed a flicker of luminous light that appeared through the cuts, but only for a moment. It was so dark, but the little bit of light enabled me to gauge its size. The amazing thing was that, as large and powerful as it was, it was subject to me and could do nothing while I took authority over it.

I knew I was on an assignment given by God on behalf of Will. Will was someone I got to know while we were in the same bay, and we became good friends. However, I did not understand what significance this had with what was going to take place later on that morning. After having so many surreal spiritual experiences, I was trusting God that was another one and something important, even though I did not understand fully. I believed, but only just. Most people would put those kinds of experiences down to someone hallucinating or being 'one slice short of a loaf of bread'.

Spiritual experience cannot be understood with the logical mind. The spirit of the man needs to be awakened and alert to realise them. However, to be awakened is not a simple matter. Once you are aware of the spiritual world, it also becomes aware that you are aware. You are bombarded with the knowledge, secrets, suggestions, torments, fears, challenges and visitations that are too much for the logical mind. If you are not covered by God, your spirit is like bait, waiting to be captured, possessed, and held captive. It could cause one to be paralysed with fear.

Anyone who enters this reality will belong to one of two camps. There is the kingdom of light where Jesus is the head with ministering angels and those men and women who accept him as their personal saviour. Or there is the kingdom of darkness where Lucifer is the head with the fallen angels, demons, and men and women who worship him.

The fight is for the souls of men. The kingdom of light is about saving souls from hell, but the kingdom of darkness is about capturing souls for hell. Sadly, there are people who are not conscious of this reality and are oblivious to plans, strategies, and schemes designed to pull them in one or the other direction. However, it impacts our lives without us knowing. Our free will and what we choose to do have a massive impact on what happens in our lives and with our loved ones.

Being unaware of the spiritual world is like going into a room and only seeing two doors. That's what the logical mind understands; it can't see anything else and, as far as it is concerned, anything else does not exist and therefore can't trouble you. Being aware spiritually is like going into the same room and seeing the two logical doors as normal, but also seeing a third door that does not make any sense (because it's not logical), but it's there. Once it is opened, your life will no longer be the same. A door allows two states: you're going into another dimension and that reality is now coming into yours. You will see things that cannot be explained, but you know about. You will understand things that you've never learned, but they make sense to you but are nonsense to others who are not aware. This reality is far greater, more complex, than the one we know. In fact, our reality is just a blip in comparison.

After the experience with this gigantic demon, my spirit returned to my body on the bed and I went to sleep. But for the rest of the morning, I was tormented with a name that kept waking me up. It was ringing in my head: Cronus! Cronus! Cronus! It bothered me so much that, as soon as it was light, I got up and went surfing the web for this name that prevented me from sleeping. I found the name meant 'Timekeeper'. From ancient Greek mythology, Chronos was a God, the father of time. I sat in my bed and tried to make sense of the experience and the name ringing out in my head.

It dawned on me, as a computer systems analyst, that "cron" is the name of a program used to schedule programs, controlling them to start at specific times. In essence, a timekeeper. I understood that Will's time was up and that he would not come back from theatre. I was sure that what I did was to ensure that his operation would be a success.

Later on that morning, when everyone was waking up, Will called me and asked me to read Psalm 91 for him. I said, "Just before I read the psalms, I want to pray with you. Is that OK?"

"Sure," he replied.

I said a simple, straight-to-the-point prayer. As I was praying, I touched him in the same areas. I cut the demonic spirit and ended the prayer in the authority of the name of Jesus. I then read Psalm 91 to the end.

About forty minutes later, the nurse came and gave him his theatre gown. Ten minutes on, the anaesthetist came to do a pre-check. He went to Will's bedside and introduced himself. It was a different anaesthetist whom Will had never met.

He said, "Morning Will. Are you ready for your operation?"

"Yes, I am," replied Will.

"I just need to go through your historical record before we proceed."

He started looking at Will's medical details. After a while, he had a concerned look on his face. He said, "You've only got 30 percent lung capacity. That is cutting it fine. Your blood sugar levels are very high and are not under control. This is very serious. On top of that, you're already taking morphine."

He concluded, "No. No. I'm cancelling this operation with all the things that I have pointed out to you. If we take you into theatre, we will lose you. We can't give you any more morphine, and your blood sugar levels could cause you to go into a coma. We need to get your blood sugar levels down and under control and improve your lung capacity."

He went away, and Will was very upset.

At that point, I felt like an idiot, believing that the out-of-body experience was all to do with helping Will go through his operation safely. I started talking to the Lord in prayer. I was very confused, unsure, and began to doubt all that I had been experiencing.

I said, "Lord? What was all that about? I'm having these far-fetched visions and dreams that I'm struggling to believe as it is! And, just when I'm coming to terms with it all, I get this weird experience that I thought was to help Will have a safe operation, and it's cancelled!"

I was very serious and worried that I was going mad. I needed some answers and reassurance. I continued with my complaint, "Lord? This isn't helping my faith. If you want me to believe what I'm experiencing is real, it has to make some sense."

I wanted an answer and some reassurance that I was not going mad.

While I was complaining to the Lord, I could hear Will on the phone with someone. I believe it was his pastor. I heard him say. "Pastor, my operation has been cancelled! I was not happy with the decision, but if I had gone in, I would have died!"

"I asked Irvine to read Psalm 91, and he prayed. It was God that made it so that a different doctor came to see me. He was a military one. He did a thorough check and cancelled the operation. That has saved my life."

It was at that point the penny dropped. It suddenly dawned on me that what I did was not for Will to go through his operation safely, but to stop it because the timekeeper was coming to take his life during his operation.

I could feel the Lord smiling as he knew I now understood. At the same time, I felt foolish for complaining and my short-sightedness. I muttered under my breath, "You idiot, Irvine." The Lord had answered my questioning by allowing me to hear Will's conversation. A sigh of relief came over me. The experiences were a bit too much for me to take in, but they were very real. I repented of my doubting.

I never got the chance to tell Will at the time why I prayed when he asked me to read, and also why I touched him in the four corners of his body during the prayer. He must have wondered why.

We made the most of our time while we were in the same ward. We talked about the things we'd done and what we wanted to do. He wanted to do some missionary work in Africa. I wanted to record an instrumental album.

He turned around to me one day when we were talking in his bay and said, "You know, if this was in certain countries, we most likely would be dead with what we've been through?"

I replied, "You're right. I never looked at it that way but, yes, you're right."

It made me think deeply that I was not meant to die. Not just yet, anyway.

I lost contact with Will when he left hospital. I tried unsuccessfully to get in touch with him but was told by others who knew him that he had gone to Africa and was doing exactly what he planned to do. He was no longer in the wheelchair, either. I was happy that I heard he had made a full recovery.

Four years later, I actually got in touch with Will. Not only was he walking around and not in a wheelchair, but he looked very well. I was able to tell him what happened that day I prayed, and it felt like a burden off my shoulder.

Intensive Care

The intensive care unit was right next door to the theatre. From what I understood, it was the first port of call when you came out of theatre until you were conscious and stable. My bed was facing the staff nurse's office. To my left were the doors from theatre. There was one bed to my left and one to my right, then on the adjacent wall, were two more beds and an open area where the nurses tended to gather and talk while they were watching over us. Each bed was attended by one nurse. We all had our own nurse, whose sole responsibility was to look after us until we were moved to a normal ward. A TV was positioned on the wall, which we could all see from our beds. The nurses were watching the countdown to the new year. It was about 10 p.m. After taking my medication, I was wide awake and listening to the nurses quite intently and laughing at their jokes.

I recall watching on the TV some of the major cities around the world celebrating the passing of 2010 and the entrance of 2011. With the different time zones, we would watch these cities pass into 2011 one by one. When it came to our countdown, the staff nurses pulled out a bottle of wine, each of them with a cup. They asked me if I wanted to celebrate with them, and I said yes and joined in with the celebration from my bed. I think I was the only one who seemed well and awake enough to join in.

In intensive care, from my recollection, there were four of us: two women and two men. The other chap was older than me, and his name was Eugene. He recovered quicker from his brain operation and was moved out to a normal ward, so I did not see him until later on when I was moved out. The other two women and I were left in intensive care. I was there for two days before I was moved. But before I was moved, I had more spiritual experiences, and two specific ones I can remember.

Woman With Aneurysm

There was the woman in the bed next to mine, who had an aneurysm. It was disheartening to know that it had left her totally motionless. The only thing she could do was breathe.

Her oesophagus would become partially blocked with mucus and the nurse assigned to her would have to quickly see to her and use a suction tube to clear her airways, otherwise she would choke to death. Her family would come to see her and were filled with mixed emotions of anger, hope, and total devastation. They could not come to terms with what had happened to their mum. They were angry with the staff nurses because they did not feel they were doing enough to help her. The daughter would come along with the rest of the family members, almost in tears, but hopeful.

I could not physically see the woman because of the privacy partition between us. What the daughter was saying and the way she was talking – loud and slow – meant she was trying to stimulate her mum or get some sign of life. She would fix her mum into what she thought was a more comfortable position.

"Come on Mum. Here you go, I'll prop your bed up for you. That's better. Come on Mum, give me a smile. Try to move your arm, Mum, come on," her daughter said encouragingly. I could hear her rubbing her mum's hand while she moved her mum's arm up and down. She kept on repeating the words, "Come on, Mum, you can do it." This would last for about fifteen minutes.

I must admit, I felt annoyed, because I could not help thinking that her mum, before she was struck down with the aneurysm, was and probably is an intelligent woman. But her daughter was talking to her as though she could not understand and in a childlike manner. From having a stroke, I knew I could hear, see and understand what was said to me, but just could not respond. People often make the mistake of treating you as though you've lost all your intelligence and understanding, when really you have a physical illness. I felt she should have just talked to her mum as she would normally.

After a while, there were sounds of cheers and laughter. "There you go, Mum. I knew you could do it," the daughter said, rejoicing. The family's hope of their mother making a recovery had increased. Her mum managed to lift her arm on her own. The family felt relieved and left feeling better. After about thirty minutes, the woman started having breathing problems as her oesophagus became partially blocked. The nurse came along quite quickly and cleared her airways.

Later on that day, during another visit, the family returned to see their mum. They were clearly not happy she could not move her arm like the last time. It seemed as though she had got worse. The family did not feel the nurses had done enough. The daughter went through the same routine as last time with her mum and got the same results: her mum managed to move her arm. Once again, the family was overjoyed and then made a complaint to the nurses that they needed to stimulate her to help her to recover. After airing their views, they went home.

I began to think about what I saw and heard. The family were happy their mum could move her arm, but what if she wanted them to stay and talk to her, even though she could not respond, and reassure her that she was still their mum? I began to feel that feeling that family and friends might not treat me the same anymore. *Now that I'm ill, they'll want me to do the things that make them feel better*, I thought. *What about me? I don't want to be treated any less than I was before a tumour.* I guess I did not like how, in my mind, the family relied on their mum to move her arm for them to feel better. That's what they needed. I can't help thinking what she wanted from them to make her feel better?

After the family had gone, I fell asleep and, during that time, found my spirit travelling. My spirit could see the woman behind the partition. I heard huffing and puffing, not from her physical body, but from her spirit. I saw a very strange thing: I saw the woman physically lying on the bed, but her spirit was trying desperately to detach itself from her own physical body. No matter how hard she tried, she could not get free. Her spirit was like a glistening transparent bubble, like a form of her physical self. It tried so hard to get out and could not. The best way to describe it is her spirit was still attached to her body only by her hands and feet. When she tried to pull away, she managed to get to the point where the main part of her spirit body was separated from her physical body except her fingertips and toes. They just would not detach. If you've ever watched the movie of *Peter Pan* when he was detached from his shadow and tried to reconnect it to his physical self, it was a bit like that, but in reverse. This went on for about what seems like most of the night until daybreak. When she realised it was dawn, she gave up and stayed within her body. I heard an angelic voice say to me, "She doesn't want to live."

From what I saw through my spirit, this woman was very attractive, based on how her spirit looked. I could remember at the time quite clearly what she looked like. I was determined to get a look at her when I came back to myself to see if she looked just like her spirit looked. I needed to do it for my own sanity. There were so many spiritual encounters. Were they just wild imaginations or hallucinations?

When it was time for me to leave intensive care, I got my answer when my bed was wheeled out onto a normal ward. I had to go past this woman's bed, so I purposely sat up to look at her as I passed by, and she looked exactly how I remembered her spirit looked. It was not my imagination after all – it was real.

I never saw that woman again but, a few weeks later, she came straight back to my mind while I was thinking about her, and I heard the angelic voice say to me, "She's passed away."

The Woman Kate

In the bed adjacent to me was a woman who had a massive stroke. Apart from barely moving her arm, which was stuck in a clenched-fist position, she could not move or talk to her family. They were sitting around the bed and were at a loss. They were paralysed with despair and did not seem to know what to do or think. They were too devastated for words. I don't recall much being said right up until visiting time was over. It was very silent.

I was tired and fell asleep. The next thing I remember was being inside the kingdom of darkness again binding the strongman, then breaking the chains off a woman's legs. As I stood in the path of the strongman with my back to him, he could do me no harm, and was subject to me. I looked towards the woman and shouted, "RUN KATE, RUN!" I knew her name

– I don't know how, but I just did. All I can remember was seeing a pair of white legs running out of the kingdom of darkness before anything else could stop her. After she had gone, my spirit came back to my body, and I went back to sleep.

About thirty minutes after, I was startled awake by the woman adjacent to me. She started screaming out and talking gibberish. As she continued screaming and talking gibberish, her speech got clearer and clearer. Straight away, I recognised she was recovering from her stroke, as I recall when my speech had gone when I had a stroke. An angelic voice said to me, "She's recovering." I called out to the nurse close to me, "Is she all right?"

"We don't discuss patients with patients," was the reply. They then closed the curtains all around her.

I knew the woman I rescued from the kingdom of darkness was the woman in the bed adjacent to me. The next time her family came to visit, they were happy and smiling. The woman was talking and responding back to them, moving her head and arms as normal. The angelic voice said to me, "She's getting better."

The medical team kept me in intensive care until my condition had stabilised. I had to get used to bed baths and losing all my dignity and pride, becoming dependent on others. I could not go to the toilet because I had a catheter in, and I needed a nurse to empty it every so often. The fluid that was being drained from my head into a side bag was still red. I was heavily monitored until it became just water. To be honest, I had no worries.

My oxygen levels kept dropping, so I was on oxygen for a while. When they stopped the oxygen, my breathing would become erratic, so they would put me back on it. Apart from that, I was recovering very well. I was well looked after while in intensive care. It was time for me to move to a normal ward.

The bay I was moved to was not the one I was in originally in; someone else had taken my space in there that also needed brain surgery. Up until then, I had no knowledge or interest in what brain tumours were. I must say I was very ignorant on the matter. I thought it was a rare condition but, having been in hospital, I have seen quite a few people before and after me with tumours, and they were more common than I first thought.

The new bay was two bays down from my old bay at the end of the building. There was not as much light down as there were no windows on the corridor side.

I met new friends while in that bay. It was very social and noisy and, when I was in the other bay, I recall hearing laughter and a lot of banter with the nurses, to the point it would disturb my sleep, and now I was in that bay. We all got on and had one thing in common: we had all been in hospital for at least two weeks. We had quite a few laughs. It was where I met Will, Malcolm, Eugene and Gordon, not to mention Cheeky Chas.

Looking back, I learned a lot from the people I met in hospital. This came about from the many times I was moved from ward to ward. A new policy had come into force that ten days was the limit for anyone to stay in hospital. After that, they needed to go home or be moved elsewhere. They tried on numerous occasions to send me home when I was clearly not ready but, somehow I stayed in and they just moved me around instead. Wherever I went, I met new friends.

I recovered very quickly and looked very well. I have never been seriously ill in my life, so I was very keen to show everyone that I was well. I recall someone advising me, "Don't let the nurses or doctors know how well you are. Play it down a little."

I did not know what that meant, but I soon learned later on when I was rushed out of hospital back home with no aftercare or sound advice. The penny eventually dropped. I recall while in the high-dependency ward after another operation, my right arm was totally paralysed. I could not do much for myself; I was dependent on the nurses for washing, feeding and helping me go to the toilet, which was one thing I disliked.

I was inspired by a young woman to be independent again. This young woman I thought was about to die. I felt very sorry for her. All the time I was in this ward, she writhed with pain in her bed for days and very rarely got out. The nurses were constantly around her, attending to her needs. I didn't think there was any hope for her. She was very loud and her groans were constant and pitiful. For the rest of us in there, it was soul-destroying.

One day, I did not hear a peep out of her, and I thought she had died. To my surprise, I watched her open her closed curtains, get off the bed all smiling and make her own way to the toilet and shower cubicle area. I was shocked. I could not believe it was the same person. She seemed to recover overnight. I thought to myself; *I want to be able to do that too.*

As soon as the nurse came around to check on me, I voiced my desire. I said, "I want to do what she just did, go to the toilet by myself and sit in the chair and not lie down." I wanted to let everyone know that I was OK and getting better; my pride got the better of me to become independent again.

I'll never forget that straight look the nurse gave me when I said what I said. She said, "Are you sure? I can help you." Little did I know it became a box-ticking exercise; I can imagine what she was thinking: he can walk by himself ... tick; he can go to the toilet by himself ... tick; he can sit up ... tick. Therefore, we can move him out of high-dependency.

Needless to say, I was moved out of the high-dependency ward where I really needed to be, for the help and support, to an independently mobile ward. I watched the men in there read the papers using both their hands. How lucky they were. When they got bored or needed the toilet or showers, they got up and went by themselves. I couldn't do that; I had to press the 'need assistance' button for a nurse to help me. I once took pride in the fact that most of the men around me were always pressing this button. I didn't need to, but now my situation had reversed. I realised that there were a lot of things I could no longer do because of a paralysed arm. Watching the men was disheartening. I was mainly annoyed with myself for falling for the tick-box treatment. I made sure I did not fall for it again. It seemed to me that if you look well, sound well and tick all the boxes, you go home. That sounds very logical and straightforward at face value, but there are always anomalies, personal circumstances and the nature of the illness to take into consideration. Nevertheless, I thank the medical team who removed my tumour.

The new bay was near the end of the building, with another in the corner. Looking out towards the corridor from within the open-ended bay was a wall across from the corridor with no windows. In the previous bay there were windows in the corridor wall looking out into the gardens, allowing a lot of light in, but the new area needed the lights on to make it brighter. As you walked in, there were two windows on either side of a sink in the back wall. Very similar to my previous bay, they looked out over the hospital. In the distance, you could see the snow-covered road. On the left nearest the corridor was Malcolm's bed, with mine next to it, by the window. Eugene's bed was opposite mine. He was the chap who recovered quicker than me from intensive care. Will's bed was next to Eugene's. We got talking and exchanged information on what got us where we were.

Chapter Seven
New Friends

Eugene

Eugene had retired and was enjoying it, doing the things he wanted to do. He'd worked hard all his life and was making the most of it. He loved gardening and certain leisure activities. He was outside by his back door when he suddenly collapsed. It came as a shock to him when he went into hospital. He found out he had a brain tumour, but took it in his stride. We were both striving well in recovery and were motivating each other. He recovered quicker than me and came out of intensive care before I did. We ended up in the same ward; he was in the bed opposite mine.

We both had catheters in place. I was very wary of having it for too long in case of infections so, within a few days, I had mine taken out and was able to pass water as normal. I still had the staples in my head and the tube protruding from my skull to drain the fluid from my head. Until it became clear like water, I had to keep it in. Eugene did not seem to have one.

He was quite enthusiastic about recovering. The day I had my catheter out, he wanted his out too. When he asked about it, the nurses seemed a bit wary of it, and their hesitation made me think there was something they were not saying. He eventually had the catheter out after a couple of days, but his enthusiasm had noticeably gone. He said to me "You know what, Irvine? What happens after this?"

I replied, "You'll just have to take it easy and make the most of your retirement. At least you're not in the rat race anymore."

"Yes," he said, stretching the word as he said it, then followed by a long pause. He continued, "But that's what I was doing and then this happened."

He was not comforted by my words but went down in himself with worry and concern about what kind of a life he had left. He was disappointed that, as he should have been enjoying his retirement, instead he was coming to terms with what had just happened to him. He was struggling with this and regressed. He went off his food and could not pass water, so they put the catheter back. This caused him to go down even further. What made it worse was that he could see I was recovering rapidly, and he was not. We both were recovering at a quick pace together, but then I had left him behind.

Although it was very sad, there were some funny moments in this ward. Three out of the four of us snored very loudly, and

Eugene also talked in his sleep between his snores. You could not be sure what was going on with Eugene. He would be quite reassuring and definite in his decisions. When he slept, he would reveal all, by talking about it in his sleep differently to what he said earlier.

One afternoon when he was off his food, at lunch the food trolley came around with his meal. He refused it and said he was not hungry. The nurses insisted on him eating something, a boiled egg even, but he just flatly refused. When he fell asleep shortly after lunch, he started snoring. The rest of us were just reading or lying down and it was fairly quiet up until then. Then, out of nowhere, he started talking in his sleep between his snores and whistles. He said: "Hrrrrghhh pheeewww lunch! Hrrrrghhh boiled eggs!" He was gasping for breath as he laid flat on his back. "Hrrrrghhh I'm hungry! Pheeewww, hrrrrghhh. I really wanted to eat pheewww."

The rest of us did not know what to make of it at first. We thought it was a joke, but soon realised he was deep in sleep.

Another night, I was jolted out of my sleep by his snoring. Will and Malcolm were already awake, and Will said to me jokingly, "All that's left for him to do now is to say his account number; he's talked everything else in his sleep." We all laughed and listened — we could not exactly switch him off from snoring.

It must have been the noisiest bay. There was always chatter during the day and lots of snoring during the night. I remember one night it was so loud I could not get to sleep. Eugene had his very constant snore with talking in between, Will had a throaty snore that was there on and off, and Malcolm had the loudest and it would catch you unawares and make you jump. He would be silent for a long while then, all of a sudden, his mouth opened so wide his tongue must have fallen back too far into his throat, blocking his airways. It would be forced out with his mouth snapping shut, making a hideous noise like a wild beast. Late at night it would make you jump. His cycle was about every ten minutes.

I was awake all this time until about 12.30, when all the snoring began to quieten down and the night started to become peaceful until one of the night nurses needed to get something from the store cupboard. It was at the end of our bay. All the lights were off, so whoever it was could not see what they were doing. They walked past the bay very quietly and went into the cupboard, where they must have knocked something to the ground. It was metal, and the noise was so loud it could wake the dead. The item resonated after it hit the floor, which prolonged the noise. It disturbed all of our sleep to the point where, one by one, everyone started snoring again. I was so tired, I eventually fell asleep, but was awakened about 2 a.m., this time by my own snoring, to find that everyone else was sleeping quietly. I eventually went back to sleep.

Eugene gradually got worse and had a relapse. He suddenly sat up in bed one afternoon while he was still sleeping and fell over the left side of his bed, banging his head on the side cupboard before he hit the floor. The alarm was raised and every doctor and nurse came running to his aid. He was unconscious.

When this occurred, I was right in the middle of having the tube removed from my head, but was left with the partially removed tube exposed while the doctor attended to Eugene. I think this was the cause of the brain infection I caught later on.

Eugene was moved from our "independently mobile" ward to a high-dependency ward where the nurses could see all the patients in their bay from their desk. I don't know what became of Eugene, but I'm hoping he made a good recovery.

Cheeky Chas

I'm not sure what Chas was short for, but he was a one-off character. I thought he was one of the male staff nurses on duty by the way he conducted himself, but he was a bank staff member. The bank staff are temporary staff that are called when they are needed. He had been doing it for years. Always in a clean, sharp, blue nurses' uniform, he was a thin chap and not very tall, with a nicely trimmed beard. He seemed to spend a lot of time in our bay and was very chatty. He was a good laugh at times but was not very sympathetic to our conditions, rather making light of it and sometimes being quite insulting without realising. If any of us upset him, he would become very vindictive and wait for his opportunity to get his own back. When you got to know him, he did not seem as offensive as from the first impressions of meeting him, but I was very wary of him. He would not think twice of taking advantage of your vulnerability if it meant he could get his own back.

One morning Chas came in and was ranting and raving, giving verbal abuse to Malcolm, accusing him of eating his sandwich.

"Malcolm, did you eat my sandwich?" He raised his voice accusingly.

"No, I don't know what you're talking about," replied Malcolm, who was a little confused. He was in again to have his third brain tumour removed.

"Yes, you did!" said Chas very sharply. "What did you have?" Chas continued.

"A tuna sandwich," replied Malcolm. You could see the expression on his face as he sat in bed almost saying, "Why are you asking me this? It's got nothing to do with you."

"THAT was my sandwich! You did not order it. I did!" snarled Chas, and stormed off, muttering things under his breath. Malcolm turned to the rest of us, raised his hands and eyebrows, and said, "What's his problem?" Needless to say, he was hostile towards Malcolm for the rest of his shift.

Will later called me and said, "Irvine, you see Chas. He's not very nice, you know. A few people have complained about him."

I replied, "I think he went overboard a little with Malcolm. Why would Malcolm eat his sandwich, anyway? We order ours from the menu the night before. Where did he leave his?"

"That's the point: he's not supposed to order a sandwich. He keeps doing that. He should bring his own food in."

I realised what he was saying. Chas was sneakily ordering his breakfast on the patients' menu without anyone knowing, as a spare, so that when it would obviously be left, he would take it. On that occasion, it must have been given to a new patient on another ward, and Chas blamed Malcolm.

Chas, by now had upset or annoyed most of us in the ward for one reason or another so, one breakfast time as I was making my way to the showers, coincidentally I walked past the food trolley. I noticed Chas coming out of one of the side wards off the corridor ward and followed the food trolley. On impulse I shouted jokingly, "Chas, there's nothing on the trolley for you today." He turned towards me with that vindictive look on his face. He did not like my comment and knew what I was getting at. I knew he was going to pay me back, and he came rushing towards me at a very brisk pace. I tried to get to the showers before he got to me, but I could not walk quickly enough. I was not going to make it in time but, luckily, there was a toilet cubicle I could get to. I could not move very fast, but I just about got in there and locked the door before he arrived.

I stayed in there for about five minutes. I could see a shadow under the door and knew he was there. He did not know that I knew he was still there. He knocked on the door several times as though it was someone checking on me to see if I was OK. He never spoke, and neither did I. I stayed in there for a further ten minutes before I noticed the shadow had gone. I sat down on the toilet seat for a further five minutes, as my legs began to get weak.

When I knew it was safe, I carefully opened the door and checked no one was around. I popped my head around and looked up and down the corridor. I could not see Chas. I looked in the direction of the showers, where I was originally heading. The door was open, so I knew no one was in there, so I made it as quick as I could to get in, just in case he was watching out for me. By the time I came out, Chas had finished his shift.

Malcolm

Malcolm was a tall man in his late sixties with a full head of hair. He looked younger, and you'd never believe he'd gone through three brain operations removing tumours over the past twenty-five years. His first was when he was in his early forties, at the front of his head. You could not see any scars because of his full head of hair. He was very pleasant, but got confused from time to time. He was due to leave hospital the week I came into the ward, but became upset when they told him he could not go, because they found out he had developed a brain infection. He was put on a drip until it had cleared up. It was something I became familiar with later on when I went through the same experience.

He was very orderly, up early every morning to the showers, and his clothes were always in a nice, neat pile at the bottom of his bed. The area around his cubicle was always kept in order until we noticed something was wrong when he kept repeating himself. He would keep reminding us that he was going home that day and refold his clothes at the bottom of the bed, waiting impatiently for his wife to come and collect him. The thing is, Malcolm had been told several times he was not going home, but he would forget and become confused and annoyed.

During visiting hours, his wife came, as she came around the corner to his bedside, Malcolm sat up holding the drip stand and straight away said, "Where have you been? What's taken you so long? You know I need to get home."

She replied, "You know I always come during visiting hours. What time did you expect me to be here? And no, you're not going home today. You've been told 100 times you need to stay in until your infection clears up."

She managed to calm him down. She fussed around him, collecting his worn clothes and exchanging them for some fresh, clean ones, changing his socks while he sat on the bed, arms folded. This did the trick. But, as soon as she would leave, he'd forget what she told him and remind us all again that he was going home.

When Malcolm was not confused, he was a humorous person. We had a few laughs, but he was very impatient with the nurses and would disappear for one of his long walks, dragging his drip stand with his arm attached to the drip bag. No one knew where he went until a nurse found him wandering outside the hospital, halfway down the road. She brought him back inside. He did not feel the cold and did not sleep with his blanket on, as he was always hot. He did his disappearing act quite regularly.

I realised the restriction of being on a drip three times a day for up to one hour was tedious and he could not cope with just sitting there. Going for a walk would help pass the time.

We got talking one day, and I asked him, "How long have you been in, Malc?"

"It's three weeks now, but I'll be going home on Monday. That's what they told me."

I knew he was not going home on Monday, but did not comment. I questioned him, "What are you in for?"

"Oh, this is my third operation to remove another tumour they found."

"How did they, or you know you had another one?"

"They found me unconscious at a traffic light crossing with a gash to my head. I don't remember what happened, but I was told by someone who saw me that my leg gave way. I collapsed to the floor and banged my head. Because of my track record with tumours, they did an MRI scan and found this tumour. It's been taken out," he replied, moving his hair out of the way so I could see the scars.

"What about you?" he asked me.

"I have just had a tumour out, too. It's non-cancerous, but I did not know I had one either until I had a stroke. When I came into hospital, like you, they did an MRI scan and found the tumour."

I told him about how I commanded the sickness to leave my body and the stroke left my body. I don't know whether he believed me or not, but I told him anyway.

We continued chatting for a while and found out we were both from the same town and he owned the very cake shop my mum and dad always bought their cakes from when I was a child. I knew the shop well. My parents and my older sisters knew them well. He used to work for an electricity supply company and also worked part-time in the shop with his wife. After his second tumour, he had to give his main job and worked full time in the shop, mainly doing the deliveries. He could not do the deliveries anymore, so his wife had the gigantic challenge of looking after her husband and the shop. I felt for them.

When I came out of hospital, I went to visit him at the shop. Neither he nor his wife were there, just the staff. When I enquired about Malcolm, I was told he was very poorly and they hadn't been seen for months. It was so sad because it was about a year later that I went to visit, but I don't think he fully recovered from his third operation and brain infection.

Gordon

Gordon was a very interesting character. He was definitely confused after his operation. He could not remember sometimes what he did in the last ten minutes and was constantly retracing his steps and questioning himself about if he did or did not do what he had just done. He would give us all a charge, first to remind him who we were, but not to tell until he first tried to remember. He was afraid to take a shower because of what he went through, so his odour was a bit of a challenge for someone with an acute sense of smell.

He was in the bay next door to where I was. His curtain was always fully drawn back, with him sitting in the chair in a dressing gown. As anyone walked past his bed, he would call out to them with one hand to his forehead and the other stretched out towards you, clicking his fingers, trying to remember your name.

"Don't tell me, don't tell me. Errm," he would stall for time, trying to recall the name of whoever it was walking past. They would stand there and wait. If he remembered he would feel good, and the person would comment something like, "Well done, you remembered." But often he did not remember and the person standing there would say whatever their name was.

He would then give them a ticking off with a smile, "I told you not to remind me," and then start going through his thoughts again.

It was sad to see, but this was his way of trying to cope and keep control of himself. In doing so, he also tried to control others, which was eventually noticeable. He would eventually give us all the responsibility of helping him remember and then make us feel bad when we did not do what he asked us to do. After a while it made me weary, so each time I walked past his bed and we went through the memory routine, somehow, he always remembered my name, but he would still say to me, "Irvine, remember, you got to remind me to concentrate, concentrate."

I replied, "Gordon, you need to remind yourself. You can't rely on others to do it for you."

From then on he always wanted to talk to me. He seemed to value my opinion. He would tell me his worries. I got to know him a little and tried to help him as much as I could.

One day, as I was walking back to my ward, Gordon was heading towards me with his mobile phone in one hand and his other scratching his head. He said, "Irvine, you've got to help me."

I replied "OK. What's the problem?"

He quietly looked around and made sure no one could hear, pulled me to one side and said, "I know it's wrong, but I have got two girlfriends on the go. They don't know about each other and I can't remember which one I have just called and now I need to call the other one."

I did smile to myself and wondered how he was going to cope with two women and memory problems. Also, what advice was I going to give him?

He continued, "You see, Irvine, I don't know which will stay with me. I know I have got to say bye to one, but I don't know which one. Will any of them want to stay with me?"

"I think the first thing you need to do, Gordon, is concentrate on your health and recovery. The least of your worries is which girl to call. The one who stays with you after the truth comes out will most likely be the one who loves you. But if not, you need to focus on getting better."

I thought it was a good answer. Gordon began to tell me more. "I never had problems, Irvine. I was a very successful sales manager and did not have time for problems. I was constantly on the road. Whenever I had problems, I just threw money at it. Job done. That's how I was until I became ill."

He unravelled so much about himself that I began to build up a picture and understood a little about where he was coming from. "Money answered everything!"

Because he was wealthy, he had girlfriends and a lifestyle that made him a little overconfident, some would say arrogant. Money was his weapon. The way he tried to control us in the bays, it was not hard to imagine him in his prime – he was very controlling and got his own way. But he was struggling to keep that command and control of his world. His illness was a big blow. Now that he had ill health, he wanted to do the right things in his life and be a little friendlier, but it had to be done with some urgency. He wanted to right the wrongs. He realised that money was not everything and, when your health is at stake, those who are not true friends don't stick around.

Any one of the two girlfriends, I believe, apart from his money, were among the remaining important areas in his life. He was anxious about what was going to happen if one or none was going to be around when they found out about him.

I did not see Gordon after a while. He was soon discharged from the hospital and I never knew if his memory improved or what became of his predicament.

Chris

After Gordon was discharged, another gentleman came into the ward in the bed next to where Gordon was. I did get used to being friendly, so I would go around and talk to others in the other bays.

I got talking to Chris, and we exchanged our stories of why we were in hospital. I did not know much about him. He seemed a very active, 70-year-old man, but he had a back problem that prevented him from doing anything. He was lying down most of the time.

What struck me was what he said to me. Not knowing much about me, he began, "Irvine, you know what? I have learned a lot since being in here. It sometimes takes something drastic to happen to you before you realise what's important in life."

"That's true," I replied.

He continued, "There are some people who I need to treat better and acknowledge that they have always been there for me in my life, when I'm better and I get out of here. I realise I have taken some things for granted."

As if on cue, this elderly lady came up and started making a fuss over him. She packed away some nice and neatly ironed pyjamas, clothes and slippers in the cupboard. She put a selection of fruit and drinks on top of the cupboard. She was his wife. She never said a word, and he looked at her and never said a word. I perceived that he wanted to thank her but did not know how to. He seemed uncomfortable with showing his softer side to his wife, who was looking after him very well. I knew instantly that one of the first people he was going to thank and show more appreciation to was his wife.

Confused Man

Another man I did not get to know took the bed where Gordon was. I don't think he was old in age, but he looked old. After he had his tumour removed, he was in his own world; he did not engage with anyone and did not seem to be recovering well. He had memory problems and kept getting up with his walking stick and hurriedly walking off down the corridor. A nurse would bring him back, he would sit there for twenty minutes then do the same thing again. He kept on insisting he had to go somewhere. He did this all the time he was in the hospital. I don't recall him having any visitors, but it looked like hard work for the nurses trying to keep tabs on him in case he wandered off somewhere he should not be. It was so sad to see. I can only imagine his memory was stuck in a loop and he could not get out. He just kept on repeating the same actions.

There was also a young man who looked like someone in his late twenties who also had a tumour removed. He just walked around the ward confused, struggling to come to terms with his condition, as if to say, "What has happened to me? Why?"

I never realised how many people are affected by brain tumours and the impact it has on their lives and loved ones. Not all make a full recovery.

With these two men, I did not see any visitors come to see them.

Steve

I met another man, called Steve, walking past me back to his ward as I was coming back from a walkabout. I noticed his walk straight away, as it was very similar to how I was walking after I had a stroke. I stopped him and asked what happened and he told me he had a tumour removed, but it grew back, and the second time they removed it he had a stroke and it left him with a shuffle walk and a weakness on his right side. His tumour was still growing back. I was mortified that his tumour was still growing. He was very calm about it and told me in a very cheerful manner. I could not help but wonder how he was really feeling inside, knowing that.

Brian

Brian was a man I met the second time I was admitted to hospital. He was on the same medication as me. He also had a tumour, but had other complications. He had lost a lung through lung cancer a few years before and now had the brain tumour. He had extreme mood swings and had threatened one of the staff nurses just before I got there. As usual, I introduced myself to all the other men in the bay and explained what my condition was. They also exchanged their stories. In particular, Brian's story was a very sad one. We got talking and got on so well. He got a lot of comfort from me just listening to his own problems while he got them off his chest, so much so that he wanted me to move my bed next to his. I declined, mainly because he was not sleeping much and talked a lot. I needed to sleep as I was rushed into hospital for an immediate operation and it had been postponed until the next morning.

Before that night was over, Brian had told me his story, his anxieties and concerns for his health. He said to me, "Irvine, I have got a brain tumour, but do you know, before that I had lung cancer, so I had to have my right lung removed a few years ago. My health isn't that good."

"Oh dear," I replied.

He continued, "My wife isn't that well either. She's had a knee replacement. She can hardly walk and I can't help her."

I could tell he was distressed with his state of helplessness, blaming himself for all that had happened. I suggested, "Have you got children who could help?"

He replied, "I have two, but they can't help. You see, my daughter is married, and she's mainly with her husband's family. They are too far away. My son, he'll wash up and that's about it. He can't cook, he's a student, so she has got nobody to help."

He had tears in his eyes while he got some more off his chest. He needed someone to offload to. The nurses were wary of him and the other patients stayed out of his way; he was demanding and could get aggressive. I was told by one of the other patients that he had attacked one of the nurses. With me having been there, I would listen to him and this gave him some comfort.

He continued, "My wife laid into me verbally. She said to me, 'All these twenty-five years I have cooked and cleaned for you. I have always been there for you and now I need you. You're not there for me! You're no help. You're a waste of time.'"

Brian's facial expression said it all – he was in pain. He held on to my arm and looked into my face and said, "You know what she said? It was true, and I felt it. I could not say anything because she was right. Now I want to help her and I can't. All these years, I have done nothing for her. I have taken her for granted."

I just listened. He continued, "I did whatever I pleased. I came in whenever I did, I went out when or wherever I wanted to and she never complained. I expected the home to be looked after; my dinner was always there; the kids were taken care of. I did not have a care in the world. She never complained and continued to look after me."

His lips were quivering as he held back his tears.

I tried to be helpful by making some suggestions. "Do you have any brothers, sisters, or family who could help?"

He replied, "I have my mum and my sister, but they won't have anything to do with my wife and she doesn't speak to them either. My wife blames me for this. Again, she's right. When I was well, there was a big family bust-up between them that I could have easily sorted out, but I left it until it was too late. There is nothing I can do to help her. What should I do? What can I do?"

I was at a loss for words to help him or comfort him; I did not know what I could say to help. He was getting all worked up and frantic. The most I could say to him was, "Brian, I think you need to focus on your health right now. Getting all worked up is not going to help them or you. Concentrate upon getting better and focus on improving your health so that you can at some point go home to help her and, if you can, sort out the family bust-up. If it's not your time, you'll get a chance to right some wrongs."

"Thank you," said Brian.

His health was not very good, with only one lung and a brain tumour to contend with; he was worried about what state he would be in after surgery, if he came out at all. I could not stop him from worrying. He felt guilty about how he'd been throughout his marriage. It hit him like a ton of bricks, as the saying goes. He was afraid of dying before getting a chance to set his house in order.

I wanted to help, but there was nothing I could do to reassure him. That night I prayed a prayer for him and his family, that all would go well for him and he would get the chance to help and look after his wife, which seemed to be the main thing he wanted to fulfil.

I don't know what happened to Brian. The next day I went back into surgery for my second operation and, when I came out, I was in intensive care for a few days before moving to another ward.

Will

Will was a well-groomed man, with a very neatly trimmed goatee, smart changes of clothes every day, with pyjamas that looked like they'd just come out of the packaging. He was a God-fearing man with a lot of faith.

He was very ill, but you'd never believe it by looking at him. Because he'd suffered two collapsed lungs some years before, he often struggled to breathe properly and found it difficult to walk. His legs were wasting away, so he got around in a wheelchair. It was quite easy to forget that we were ill or about to go through an operation of some sort; being around him made you forget why we were in hospital. Our conversations were interesting and varied and felt more like a social get-together than passing time as we waited for the call. He had many visitors, especially from the church he was attending. He appeared to be well looked after.

He'd been in hospital for seven months. When he told me, I was in shock – I could not imagine staying in hospital for so long.

He said to me, "Do you know how many tablets I have to take in a day?"

"How many?"

"Fifty."

"Fifty!?" I replied, shrieking at the fact. He began to tell me what, when, and why each tablet was taken. The thought of taking so many made my throat dry. I imagined choking at trying to down fifty tablets; I became very concerned about him. I did not like taking tablets myself. The ones I had to take, as far as I was concerned, were too many. I only swallowed the ones that were not optional. I flatly refused the painkillers. I did not want to become addicted to medication and suffer from side effects.

Will was quite anxious to have his operation over and done with. He'd been waiting a long time, but the medical staff would delay it because they were patiently working behind the scenes to stabilise his health and condition. His breathing was an issue; his lung capacity was only at 30 per cent and needed to be higher. Each time they checked his oxygen intake, it was always too low and his operation was put off.

A week later, Will's condition had improved when they did the checks. His oxygen intake was acceptable, so at last the wheels were set in motion for him to go into theatre for his operation. The look on his face was a sigh of relief and dread as the reality sunk in that he was going to have surgery.

That evening Will said to me, "I can't eat anything now. It's nil-by-mouth until after the operation."

"How do you feel about it?"

"Well, I just trust God. My church and many others have been praying for me. You're also on my church's prayer list."

"Wow, thank you," I said. "You're also on my church's prayer list."

"Thank you. I need as much as I can get," Will said.

He went and told Malcolm. "Finally, you can get to go home afterwards," replied Malcolm.

"I'm going home at the end of the week," stated Malcolm.

"Oh, are you?" I enquired.

"Yes, I should be off the drip tomorrow and then I'll be on the tablets, so by Friday I can go home."

This time Malcolm was right. He did not seem as confused as before – he was getting better.

"It looks like I'll be the only one left then at this rate," I said, moaning.

Will had made a few calls to family and friends, informing them of his situation. I sat up in my bed, reading a book, until I felt tired. I put my book down after about twenty minutes, then turned to the side to go to sleep. I just kept thinking about taking fifty tablets in a day.

Huntley

Huntley was an old family friend from when I was a child. I had not seen him for over fifteen years. To be honest, he was my eldest brother's friend, so I did not really know him that well because I was just a little boy to him back then. I was surprised he even remembered me. On one of the occasions I was out of hospital, at home, sat up in bed, Del had popped in from work at midday to check on me. She ran up the stairs and said, "Irv, there's a Huntley downstairs who has come to see you. Are you OK for him to come up?"

"Huntley?"

"Yes, you must know him. He knows you. Well, I saw him walking up our street, when I took the kids to school this morning and saw him again just now. It's only when I pulled onto the drive he came over and asked me if I knew where you lived."

"Huntley? I can't think who that is."

"Apparently, he's been walking up and down the street for the past hour, but could not find the house. When his sister told him you were ill, he wanted to come and see you."

I was still puzzled – I did not know a Huntley. "So," I said, "what's his sister's name?"

"Fiona."

"Oh, I know, it must be Huntley!" It suddenly dawned on me who it was, but why did he want to see me?

"So, you do know Huntley then?"

"Yes, I do, but he was not really my associate; he was my older brother's mate. Why would he want to see me? I have not really been acquainted with him or seen him for years," I said with a puzzled look on my face.

I must admit, I was intrigued to know why he walked up and down my street, determined to see me.

Huntley was strong, stocky and very broad, but gentle. I sat up in bed and made myself comfortable while Del went back downstairs to fetch him. The stairs creaked louder and louder as they reached the top, and Del pushed the bedroom door open and said, "Here's Huntley."

Del turned to Huntley and said, "Huntley, he can't stay up for too long; he should be resting."

"That's OK, I won't be long. I have got to get back into town for an appointment," Huntley replied.

Del pulled up a chair next to the bed for him to sit on and we shook hands and then he sat down.

"My God! It's a long time since I have seen you," I said.

"I know, but I had to come and see you. I was so shocked when I heard you were ill. Of all the people, you were the last person I would expect this to happen to," he said, making himself comfortable.

His statement alone humbled me. Why not me? What was so special about me?

"Well, that's how it is in life," I replied. "You never know when things are going to hit you. When they do, you have to just deal with it the best way you can. Why not me, anyway?"

"Because you're a good person."

He thinks I'm a good person. How would he know? I thought. *He doesn't really know me, so how can he think that?* I was flattered by what he said and really appreciated him coming out of his way to encourage me.

Huntley lifted my spirits that day and left me with some very uplifting advice. He was very encouraging and let me know that I was valued and people did care.

Pastor Peterkin

On another occasion, Pastor Peterkin came to my house to see me.

Pastor Peterkin was a senior pastor in his eighties! When I was a youth, I used to visit the church he pastored in Dudley. When he would see me, he could never remember my name, and would get me mixed up with one of my brothers or another member from the church. He would generally say in his deep voice, "One of the Lewises."

I had not seen him for a number of years. He got my address details from a family member and called Del to tell me he was coming over. I was amazed that at his age he was still doing his ministerial duties, driving and getting around visiting people, as he was known for. Once again, I was overwhelmed that one of the senior members of the church wanted to come to see me to check on how I was doing. I was not used to all that attention. *Who am I?*

I opened the front door to welcome him into my home, and the first thing he said was, "Brother Irvine, God bless you the saxophone man!"

He remembered my name and the fact I was a saxophonist.

"God bless you, pastor. I'm privileged to have you in my home. Come in."

He came in with a few bags full of healthy groceries and gifts. "These are for you."

"Thank you. I'll put them in the kitchen," I replied as I showed him into the living room to sit down. I came back from the kitchen and sat down in the living room with him.

"How's the family?" he asked

"They are doing very well; all growing up."

"How is Del?"

"She's coping, but I know she's very tired. With what she has to deal with concerning me, I'm glad I'm the sick one," I said jokingly.

Pastor looked at me and said, "You have a testimony. You're a walking miracle; you will have to go around and give your testimony."

"Yes, I know."

He took out a bottle of anointing oil and anointed my head and began to pray. In his prayer, he mentioned, in his deep and bellowing voice, "Del is feeling the pressure. She doesn't know whether to scratch her head or her foot. She thought it was

131

over, but you Lord said that you would not take him away from her but he would still be there to put his arms around her again."

I just listened and appreciated his insight.

He continued, "David said, 'Yea, though I walk through the valley of the shadow of death.' But you, Irvine, went into death and the Lord brought you out. Not many people have gone through two major operations and come out. You look like you've never been ill."

After finishing his prayer, he gave me the bottle of anointing oil that I began to use over the forthcoming months until it was finished.

"Amaris looks like her mum. You have a lovely family. How's Reece the priest?" he said humorously.

"He's fine." Again, I was deeply touched that he knew my children. I did not think he would remember them.

"I really appreciate you coming to see me with all the gifts. Thank you so much."

"Brother Irvine, it's not how much you know, it's how much you care. I could not rest until I had come to see you."

I was losing count now of the many times I had heard how much people cared. I was just blown away by people telling me how much they cared about me. I had to say something to get Pastor Peterkin to answer the questions in my thoughts without asking. I said, "I'm so privileged to have you come to visit me. I'm very blessed."

He replied, "You are a well-known, talented and a blessed man. That is one reason why people have prayed and do care."

At that point, I was thinking, *OK Lord, I hear you when you said you value me, and so do all these people. You weren't joking. I acknowledge what you've said.*

"I have a little advice for you, Brother Irvine," Pastor Peterkin began to say. "The Lord, many years ago, taught me how to get up and pray early every morning. I used to get up early to pray, go to work, go to church, but did not have much rest. I eventually had a breakdown. I was in hospital for four months. Life has taught me don't just work and pray: work, REST and pray. Make sure you rest for at least one hour in the day, even if you don't sleep. It's good for the brain."

"I receive that," I said in accepting his advice.

"Can you still play?"

"Yes, I can, but not as I could before," I said proudly.

"What has the doctor said? Is it OK?"

"Yes, they have said it's OK, but I must take it easy."

After the prayer, being anointed and advised by Pastor Peterkin, he left. I went back upstairs to rest and tried to absorb and retain all that was said.

Hospital Chaplain

I met the hospital chaplain during my third admittance to the Manor Hospital. After two operations, I went home and suddenly started having regular seizures, which I had never experienced in my life before. It was quite frightening, and I was back in hospital. I had been back and forth between the QE and Manor Hospital so many times that I began to think I'd never get out.

As I was sitting on my bed, the chaplain came to see me. She was softly spoken, and also a very down-to-earth person.

"Hello Mr Lewis. Can I call you Irvine?"

"Hi, yes," I said in a very bright and positive way.

"I'm the hospital chaplain and if at any time you need to speak to someone or you would like some quiet time, we have a little chapel just down the corridor there. Here's my card with my contact details; just give me a call if you feel you might use this service."

She saw the scar on the top of my head where I had surgery. I perceived that she was curious and wanted to talk to me. I can only imagine she also wanted to know how come I was so bright and optimistic. So, I broke the ice.

"This is my third time back in hospital. It looks as though I'm going to be in here longer than I planned," I said, leaving it open for her to ask a question or respond.

"I hope you don't mind me asking. I have noticed the scar on your head. What are you in hospital for?" she said very carefully with a smile, hoping not to offend, but wanting to know more about my illness.

I began to tell her about the stroke, rebuking the sickness, the brain tumour, the sea of prayer, etc. As I was rattling on in autopilot mode, having told my story so many times, I noticed her eyes welling up with tears.

"Sorry, I must stop you there. I'm so overwhelmed with what you've been through. You've gone through so much and to look at you, it's as though you've never been ill; you look so well," she said as she desperately tried hard to keep her composure and not embarrass herself.

"I too believe in prayer," she added. "I have a brother who also had a tumour. He is a Christian. We prayed many prayers for him and he recovered very well. He also believed in the power of prayer. But my brother-in-law, who also had a tumour, when he became ill we prayed many prayers for him too but he did not believe in God or prayer. He did not recover so well and has evident signs of his illness. Thank you for sharing your experience with me; it is very inspiring."

She smiled and dried her eyes. She left me with the chaplain contact details.

Methodist Minister

I attended a community event some years ago which church and community members had helped organise. I recall meeting a Methodist minister called Phil, who introduced himself as the new minister assigned to a local church. He was of average height, very slim, with thick, grey, streaky hair. He wore glasses and always sported a moustache of similar colour to his hair. He seemed to be a very sincere, conscientious person, very committed to his calling. We would only talk if our paths crossed. We knew of each other, but never really knew each other.

At a time when I was out of hospital, there was another one of these community events. Our paths crossed, and we began with the small talk. He said, "I haven't seen you for a while. I have noticed a scar on your head. Have you been ill?"

"Yes, I have not too long come out of hospital," I replied. I then began the whole process again of telling my story. Once again, halfway through my spiel, he interjected, "Oh my God! You're the guy on our prayer list at church. I did not realise it was you." He said the penny had dropped, and he could put a face to the name of someone his congregation had been praying for.

"We have been praying for you since we heard you were ill, only we never knew who it was. We often pray for people and don't know who they are. I never knew it was you. You have a remarkable story; thank you for sharing that with me," he said with satisfaction written all over his face. He seemed excited to go and tell his congregation someone they had been praying for was healed.

Old School friend

Lee is an old school friend going back thirty years from time to time, our paths cross. I was surprised to see him at a football tournament my son was involved in. As you do, you catch up with what is going on.

After he finished telling me about his life, I was stopped before the first words would come. He turned towards me and said,

"You know Irv, although we've not seen each other for about five years, I know everything about what's happened to you and what's been happening since. I've never known anything like it. We generally hang out at the petrol station, it's like a meeting place we see so many people, and do you know as they come and go the first question is, 'How's Irvine?' Me and Daz would be updated with the latest news about you then we would pass it on to others."

He paused for a moment, then commented, "But you look really well. Look after yourself. See you in another five years," he said jokingly.

"Yeah, you're right, take care," I replied. I imagined for a moment my life must have been the talk of the town, as though everyone was waiting in suspense. Is he going to live or die? Most could not see how I was going to recover and, if I did, what state would I be in? But most were overwhelmed with disbelief when they saw me alive and well.

One of the carers who looked after my dad saw me for the first time since being ill in the local supermarket. We were coming down the escalators as she was going up, and she shouted, "Irvine! Don't go anywhere. I'm coming back down. Wait there," she said excitedly.

We waited at the bottom of the escalators for her to go up and come back down. When she came down, she gave me the biggest hug and was in tears. I could not understand it. Why was she crying? Why would she care so much?

I only knew her through my dad, apart from that I did not really know her, but she said, "You know you've really encouraged me seeing you alive and well. I did hear about your terrible ordeal and, looking after your dad, I saw the effect your illness had on your family. I did not think you were going to make it, but I'm really pleased to see you. It's made me all emotional. I'm glad you're better."

"Thank you," I replied. "It's God's mercies, you know."

Friend's Funeral

I went to an old friend's funeral. Peter was a fly-by-the-seat-of-your-pants man. All that knew him admired him. He never had any enemies but had many friends throughout parts of Europe and was a well-travelled man. He was a naturally funny guy who was into so many things, an intellectual, self-taught in three languages, a sportsman still playing basketball at age 50. You name it, he'd been there, done it and had the T-shirt. He did not even look his age. He was not a 9 to 5 man and would've probably been the envy of most people his age. He seemed truly liberated from the rat race. He used his intelligence to make an honest living and was very successful. But right at the height of success, he died in a car crash, minutes after his basketball team won a semi-final. It was only a few months before we met for the first time in about five years. He was shocked about what I had been through, and then there I was at his funeral with a few more old friends.

George, an old college friend, was at his funeral. We started catching up on old times and talked about how sad it was that Peter died, but remembering how funny and hilarious he was, too.

"So how are you now, Irvine?" George asked as we sat around a table after the funeral. "I can see the scar on your head. I know you nearly died."

"Well, I'm still here, by God's mercies, but I will say there have been so many prayers prayed for me. I don't think I would be here now if people hadn't prayed."

I then began telling him about the vision of the sea of prayers. When I finished, he looked at me in deep thought and said, "You know what? I'm not a Christian, I don't go to church or anything like that, but when I heard you were ill, I prayed for you."

I could see that he was surprised when I mentioned that the people praying for me that I saw were not just Christians. It's almost as though he'd just realised that God actually answered his prayer for me and that I was able to tell him about it and thank him. He had one request for me, which was to look out for his brother. I said I would.

I can honestly say that I was taken aback when realised so many people cared about me and valued me that they prayed and fasted! Some I don't even know. I can understand it from my family, those who know me from my Christian circles or had some association with me. Some were not from my circles, whether as friends or from the Christian circles I'm in. They probably heard about me through a friend or, in one case, saw me once but didn't really know me, but took time out and made a personal sacrifice on my behalf.

I am more than grateful for what was done in the heavens for me. I realise how import human lives are and, if we dare to care and do something, there will be a supernatural response.

Have you ever wondered what people are thinking or experiencing when they are seriously ill, at death's door or when they're subconscious or even in a coma? Are they totally blank and oblivious, have no recall at all, or are they in a different dimension? For some people they don't remember a thing and have no memory of what they have just been through, but that's not in all cases, and certainly not in my experience. I don't recall much while under a general anaesthetic, but I do recall many spiritual encounters and out-of-body experiences.

Reflections on My New Friend's Experience

When I look back on all those people I met, I did not know what to say half the time. I tried to remain optimistic and empathised with them. Some had no hope and just succumbed to their predicament, others were hopeful and those who were like me had faith and always believed it was OK. I had too many reassurances, both spiritual and physical. I knew I was OK even though my life had come to a standstill. I can't imagine what it was like for my wife, children, dad and siblings. When I looked at others, their world had fallen apart; they were anxious, fearful and troubled, but some had prepared a mental list of wrong things they were going to make right.

The main worry I found with some of the people I met in a life-and-death situation was the acts of love they never did express. They kept it inside, instead of telling someone they were sorry, forgave them, or loved them. Then it would be to treat others with kindness, care and appreciation, to be a better person, to take their health and strength more seriously and give it priority. Lastly, to do those things they were passionate about (now!), and no longer put them off.

They had no peace and were in torment that they may have run out of time and needed more of it to accomplish all those things and the dreams they always wanted to fulfil but never got around to.

This journey was like getting on a bus against your will, and it was taking you somewhere you'd never been and did not want to go. The scary part was you couldn't get off the bus until it reached your destination. The destination for each one on the bus was a different place. Some were fortunate because their final destination was not death's door, a point of no return. Unfortunately, for others, it was the last time they were going to see their loved ones in the land of the living. If they never fulfilled their destiny, it was then too late. Whatever great invention, scientific breakthrough, life-changing idea, dream or artistic creation that should have been brought to life never lived. It would be going to the grave with the one who should have birthed it. If they had never loved, forgiven those who hurt them, been the best person they could be or done some good for someone without reward, that would be the time they would remember and have the desire and urgency to do them – but it was too late. For those who lived a fulfilled life, they would most likely not have any regrets and probably be at peace.

A life-threatening illness is a life-changing one. I re-evaluated my goals in life, my aspirations, how I treated others around me, what I would do when I got out of hospital. I did a mental, physical, ambition, family and spiritual check-up on myself.

All the things I wanted to achieve in computers, music, electronics and a business venture, I did at least attempt. I was not as successful as I wanted to be in business, but it was not for the lack of trying. I did achieve all that I wanted in electronics and computers, but music was the one thing I did put on the back burner.

For my family, I always told them I loved them, not just collectively, but as individuals. I always tried to make each one feel special. If I did not think it was important before, I sure did now. As I child, I wanted to be noticed and feel special, but that was difficult in a family of thirteen. As a young adult, my mum and dad certainly did make feel that way, though.

Chapter Eight
Quick Recovery

Brain Drain

The time came for the tube to be removed from my head. After the tumour was removed, the bone had been stapled back in place, with a long tube protruding from a little hole in my head, draining off all the excess fluid into a transparent bag that I kept at my left side. I had the catheter on my right side. Both bags were emptied quite regularly. The catheter was the first to go, some days earlier. No blood is allowed to accumulate on the brain because it could trigger a stroke or seizure, so all the fluid has to be drained until it is clear fluid. The nurse checked, and it was clear.

A doctor came that evening to remove the tube. He came around the bed with his assistant nurse and pulled the curtains halfway around. I could see straight ahead of me, which meant I was looking out at Eugene sleeping. He checked the transparent bag of fluid. It was mainly water, so he was satisfied he could now remove the tube. He removed the dressing and began to pull the tube out from my head. I could feel a sucking sensation from my head as the tube was slowly pulled out. The tube was inserted under a flap of skin and under the bone flap between the staples.

While the doctor carefully pulled the tube out, I was watching Eugene, who suddenly sat up in bed and then fell sideways to his left, crashing his head against the little storage cabinet. I was almost in shock. He never flinched. Luckily, the nurse assisting the doctor rushed over to him and pulled the emergency cord, setting off the alarm. All the nurses and doctors from near and far came rushing in to attend, including the doctor who was attending to me. They pulled the curtains around him so no one could see. He left the tube half hanging out of my head while he helped Eugene. It must have taken around forty minutes before Eugene was conscious and OK. Once he was stable, the doctor came back to attend to me. He removed the tube but left it on the floor. It was the night nurse that found it and disposed of it when she came into the bay later. Where the tube was inserted into my head was the same spot, the brain infection started.

Leaves on the Windowsill

We were all in the bay one night, getting ready to switch off and go to bed. We were having a general conversation and winding down. Earlier on that day, the ward was very warm, and we opened one of the windows at the end of the bay to let some fresh air in. Later on, it got very windy outside, so we closed the window, but it would still whistle when the wind curled in the alcove past the window. The sound it was making was so eerie, it stopped us in our flow of conversation, as if demanding our attention. There would be a pause of silence, then we would continue where we left off. It got to a point where it was so disturbing; I tried to close the window properly, but without success. Malcolm also tried, but the window would whistle every time the wind blew.

Eventually, we all nodded off to sleep. The whistling sound seemed to fade into the distance. A few hours later, I could hear the whistling sound again. It was a surreal experience, because I knew I was asleep, but my spirit could hear it.

The window was a good distance away from my bed. To get near it, I would need to get out of the bed and walk across. This whistling sound was calling me. I ignored it at first, but it kept on calling me. Even though I was asleep, my spirit sat up in the bed and left my body still sleeping. I looked over towards the window. It whistled again and called out to me. I could see something jammed in the closed window, part inside the bay, the other outside the window. Each time the wind blew, it was flapping like a small piece of cloth. I looked a bit closer, and they were like leaves. I leaned forward and stretched out my hand, pulled these leaves in from the window, and the whistling stopped. As I turned them around, examining them, they looked like oak leaves, about three or four of them.

For some reason I knew the Lord was there, so I just asked, "What are these, Lord?"

He answered, "These are people's ministries."

"What am I doing with them, and why have they come to me?"

He said, "People have sent them to you to release them into ministry."

"Why me?"? I had a puzzled look on my face.

"Because you have been given that authority. Not all of them are for good," said the Lord.

I looked at the first leaf. It looked good, and I discerned it was a ministry with good intentions; it was not for self-glory but for the Lord. I knew I could release this one, but I did not know how to.

So, I asked the Lord, "Can I release it?"

"Yes."

"What do I do?"

"Let it go."

So, I held it up slightly and let go of it. The wind blew, and it fluttered away like a butterfly straight back to the person who sent it. They were now released for ministry.

I got the next one, looked at it. I was about to ask the Lord again what to do, but I perceived that he wanted me to get used to using the authority he had given me by myself. He knew that I knew what to do, but I had to discover this for myself.

Each time I discerned a good one, I released it. It went straight back to the owner and they would be released for ministry. I came across one that I could see clearly. The person who sent it wanted me to release them, but they did not have good intentions. They wanted to excel in ministry for self-glory, so I did not release it. It never went back to the owner, so that ministry was never released. I could not help wondering what happened to those who were released, and those who weren't. How did it work? Why have I got this authority? Who am I? It raised a lot of questions, but I believed and accepted what the Lord had said to me, even though I did not understand.

When I had finished, my spirit lay back down into my body.

Chapter Nine
Going Home

———————

The time had come for me to go home. My operation was a success, and I wanted everyone to know I was well and back to normal – even though I was not. I still had staples in my head and consumed a mix of medical drugs to keep me going. However, I was in good spirits and recovered very quickly, to the point where it was to my detriment. If the hospital had its way, I would have been sent home two days after the tube was removed. That was not practical; I needed the staples removed beforehand.

Apprehension took hold of me, as I did not know what my life was going to be like when I got home. It dawned on me that I would be going home. I had mixed feelings.

On the 8th of January 2010 my mum passed away. A year later, on the 7th of January 2011, I came out of hospital in time to attend my mum's memorial. I was rushed out with the advice, "Take it easy and rest." I had no physiotherapy or proper aftercare. I can only imagine, because I recovered so quickly and that I appeared very well, they didn't need to do any more. My expectations were not managed. I thought I was back to normal and was not made aware of the risks surrounding post-op brain surgery patients.

My wife, children, and siblings were relieved when I finally got home. They almost thought there was going to be a second death in the family in the space of one year.

Once they knew I was coming out, they all gathered at my home to celebrate our mum's memorial and me coming home. We had a celebration party at my house, which was full. Every room was packed with my brothers, sisters, their children and children's children. I was in a good mood. I stood along the wall against the radiator in the dining room, midway between the two doorways. A feeling of contentment and satisfaction is the best way I can describe the moment when I looked around me and saw smiling faces and so much joy. I was pleased.

The temperature was high inside but very cold outside. The front door and the kitchen door were opened to let some cool air flow through the house from the front to the back via the dining room. I stood in the midst of the flow.

I did not realise how quickly I had become accustomed to the hospital sleeping pattern, and by 9 p.m. I was ready for bed. Not only that, but I began to feel ill and needed to lie down. The party had barely started, but I disappeared upstairs and went to bed. It was also my first night on a reduced intake of a steroid known for its terrible side effects if used for more than two weeks. I did not realise how much my easy-going, laid-back ways had changed. All of a sudden I became irritated and impatient with the happy noise that a few moments ago made me smile. I tossed and turned in torment from the noise coming through the bedroom door from every room in the house. I could not take it anymore, so I got up and went to my daughter's room and told all those who were in there to keep the noise down. I marched all the little children who were causing mayhem on the stairs down to their parents, then went back to bed. About fifteen minutes later, which felt more like forever, I got up again and went to those in my daughter's room and sent them downstairs. I called Del and instructed her not to let anyone upstairs. Even though this was done, I was still tormented by the noise coming from downstairs.

Withdrawal Symptoms

As I lay in bed, all down my back and right shoulder especially, I had a burning itch, and no amount of scratching would ease the discomfort. When I tossed and turned, it would go away for about one minute, then it would start again. To make it worse, I was hot and literally soaking wet, but freezing cold. Also, I felt like I was suffocating. It was as though there was no oxygen in the air. I felt like I was going to die. I could not see no way out; there was no ease or comfort. I just concentrated on each breath to stay alive. I was at the point of panic.

I prayed and said, "Lord, my life is in your hands. If you don't help me breathe, then I'll die. Help me Lord."

I don't remember anything after that other than what seemed like six hours later, when I gradually woke up. There were no more cold sweats. Everyone had gone home. I was warm and dry but facing the wrong way in the bed.

I went through this drama each night for about two weeks with the same symptoms: irritation, tormenting itch, breathing but suffocating, the cold sweats, at the point of panic and wondering if I was going to make it. I dreaded going to bed at night; as soon as I lay down, the itching and suffocating feelings would start. My thoughts went back to Brian – his behaviour and mood changes coincided with when the steroid dose he was taking was reduced. When I woke up in the morning, I was relieved that I got through it, but my only thoughts were about getting through the next night. At the time, it seemed endless, and it was not going to stop. I took it one day at a time.

I took comfort in the little prayer I would say each night. It gave me peace and calmed me down. I did not know if I was going to sleep or even wake up. I would wake up the same way, not knowing when the torment ceased.

Chapter Ten
New Name & Character

While in the QE for the second time, I was lying in my bed in a deep sleep trying to find the answer to the question about the number 7 that May had told me about. It was then the Lord said to me that my name is "Caljah the mighty worshipper and Prophet" in one statement. I got up from my deep sleep, grabbed my pen and wrote it down, and went back to sleep. Before dosing off, I remember thinking "That sounds like a girl's name" and felt funny about it.

When I got up the next day, I tried to ignore what happened during the night, but something was bothering me. I had to look at what I had written during the night "Caljah?" I said to myself I knew it was my name, but I struggled with it because it sounded like a woman's name. I daren't question or challenge it, because by now I learned to listen and obey when God speaks, if I understood it or not. I put the name in my phone and kept it a secret for months I was uncomfortable about it until 25/03/2011 around 2am while meditating on God I blurted out a question "What does it mean anyway!?" and the Lord said to me that it means "Pure in heart". I remember from the bible in St Matthew chapter 5 verse 8 it states the "pure in heart shall see God". The Lord also said to me,

"I (the Lord) will be poured out from you when you minister, every good that you do is an opportunity to be rewarded in heaven". I was totally humbled. It stopped me dead in my tracks. I felt honoured that I had a name with such a significant meaning. I could not take it all in, it was too much for my rational mind. If I had not experienced spiritual encounters before, I would have seriously thought I was going mad.

On the 18/09/11 the Lord gave me the spelling. It's written as "Caljah" but pronounced "Carla". The "J" is silent, more like "Y". From then onwards I started bit by bit to use it, and tell others about it, sheepishly at first, but as time went by, I became more confident and proud of my name. I have noticed the more I embrace my name, the more I become it, but whenever I use my normal name, I begin to revert back to the old me.

My phone's name is Caljah; it comes up on my WhatsApp. On the 7/08/2016 my work colleague asked me, "Hey Irvine what does Caljah mean?" pronouncing the "J" as in "Jay"

I said "It means pure in heart,"

He asked, "why is it on your phone?" I told him how I got the name and why it's on my phone.

He then replied, "Oh ok, I was just wondering because in Hindi and Bengali it means heart". I was totally surprised, but it was a confirmation for me.

I also looked up the Hebrew meaning of the name, the closest spelling I found was "Calah"[6] which means full of age. In my understanding it signifies maturity by having a clean heart and mind, not allowing impure thoughts to remain but a constant cleansing keeping in line with the word of God.

I love to worship in music on my saxophone so I could readily accept the mighty worshipper statement; however, I did not know how this was going to be possible after a major illness. I wanted to play even more than before, but I could barely hold the sax with how weak I was, a lack of strength, control of my right arm and hand. I could not play fast anymore. I was lacking control and the skill I had before. For a while my right ear was hearing sounds a semitone lower than my left ear. I found this out by accident. I was playing a set with a band; they were to the right of me, so I heard everything through my right ear. Every time I played a note, it just sounded totally wrong and out of key with the singers. I would turn towards the band where I could hear them clearer through my left ear, I was a semitone out, when I adjusted to the right key it sounded spot on, the minute I turned my head so my right ear was getting all the sound again it sounded out of key again, I

---

[6] The meaning of the name Calah is found in the book "A dictionary of Scripture Proper names" by J.B. Jackson

did not know which ear was telling me the truth. This condition did not last very long. While it was evident, I was very dissatisfied with my playing I would only play in my bedroom.

I came out of hospital with a torn rotary cuff muscle; I did not have the strength to hold my sax firmly, but I could rest it on my leg and get away with that. It was a definite challenge.

As a prophet I also knew that in the past the lord has spoken, revealed things to me, through me for others either after a request for prayer, in a vision or dream or dynamically. Sometimes the revelation is clear. Most times I don't understand, but the recipient does. It is very similar to what I have read about biblical prophets.

I often wonder what it all means. How will it pan out? Living up to the full meaning and purpose of my name. What sort of character am I? How will I sound as a musician with limited ability? All of this is yet to be fulfilled.

Chapter Eleven

Reality Check

I suffered a stroke caused by a brain tumour, followed shortly after by a brain infection. After the second surgery to clean up the infection, I was left with a paralysed right arm. It did not stop there! When I regained the use of my right arm, I discovered I had a tear in the rotator cuff muscle in my right arm and, not long after, I began suffering with seizures. My whole right side was weak. I was no longer independent as previously; I had lost some cognitive and motor skills. For many years I could not pick up a glass of water to drink without spilling it, and that was just one of the many things I could no longer do. This was very difficult to accept. I did not accept it, but had to learn the hard way to be patient in recovery.

If anyone would have told me I would have a stroke, a brain tumour and a metal plate in my head, I think I would have laughed and stated, "Not likely!"

However, the whole experience was humbling and caused me to have a different perspective on life and what's really important.

The Power of Prayer

I never knew how powerful prayer could be. I have always believed in prayer, but actually feeling the effects of prayer and seeing the results for yourself is a totally different experience. It's on another level. If you thought only certain types of people can or should pray, well, I would say you will be totally surprised, as I was. When people come together, no matter who they are, where they're from, what race, creed, colour, etc. and come together and pray in unity for a good thing, those prayers will be answered, as in my experience.

Positive Thinking

Despite my helpless situation, especially on dark days, I always had hope and believed the situation I was in was only for a time. It wouldn't be long before I was back to normal. That kept me going in the long-term. Until one day, when I had the news that I needed to be on a drip ASAP to treat the brain infection. All my veins had shut down, and the doctors tried without success to find one. I gave up and thought, *This is it!* The minute my thoughts became negative, all I saw in front of me was darkness and death. I had no more answers and could not help myself. My life began slipping away faster than pouring water out of a drinking glass. Had my wife not acted quickly for a call to prayer, I would not be here now. I realise the importance of positive thinking and the need for uplifting people around you; it gives hope and breeds optimism and a better attitude when facing life-threatening situations. In my case, the brain infection, if not treated in time, would have led to paralysis and death.

I was brought up in a Christian home and became a Christian at the age of 17. I spent many weekends in church meetings being taught about God. The most important thing I found was having a personal relationship with God – my unseen but very present friend, protector, advisor, teacher, saviour and Lord. Looking back, I see how I got out of some predicaments, such as when I ran in front of a car which should have sent me flying in the air but, somehow, I put my hand on the bonnet and pushed myself over and around it, much to the amazement of the onlookers. It was as though someone unseen took the force out of the impact, so I was not injured. Some people would say I had luck on my side, but I know that it's because I had God on my side.

Having a near-death experience, I saw things and have been places through out-of-body experiences that I could not explain, but it made me become more aware there is more to life than the eyes can see. I perceived from the supernatural experiences I encountered that God values every human life and wants us to have a fulfilled life according to our true purpose and destiny, using the gifts and abilities we have. He respects our free will in what we choose. In contrast, there is a strong opposing force that is hell-bent on preventing us from knowing our true worth and value to God by using miseducation, lies and deception. It makes me wonder who are we, really?

The threat of losing my independence or, even worse, my life, made me re-evaluate what life was really about? Why am I here? What is my purpose? How long will I live?

I spent the majority of my life making sure I had a good career so I could have the lifestyle I wanted, only to find I was working flat out and not having much time to enjoy living. I did not appreciate how important it is to look after your body through work, rest, and play. I mainly worked and did not have time for the other two.

Now I wake up every day and appreciate that I'm alive. I can see the day and the beauty of my environment. Seeing my family, I enjoy the simple things like walking, breathing, smiling, watching the swaying of the trees in the wind, people going by and everyday life things happening. I'm so blessed that I'm alive to see these things and to participate in them. My daily thought is, "Every day is a good day!"

The Care and Care For

One other thing that I'm sure some people who have gone through some serious illness forget or take for granted is the carer! The term I use is the 'carer, and the cared for'. Often there is a disparity in understanding what needs to be done between the two, with lots of heated discussions, misunderstandings and plenty of frustrations. The cared for wants to fiercely maintain their independence even though they are dependent. Certainly, they do not want the carer to do everything for them. The carer doesn't like to see the cared for struggle and will try to help them. Frequently, they find their help is not welcome, yet the cared for needs the carer.

If it were possible, the carer would need to be a mind reader. I don't do dependent, and tried everything in my ability to be independent. However, when I was left to get on with life, often I felt nobody cared. I could not have it both ways! The carer (my wife) tried to care for me, but a lot of times I would push her away, so she would leave me well alone. Now I, the cared for, would struggle to cope and begin to feel uncared for. My wife was beginning to feel taken for granted and to see me as self-centred and uncaring about how my situation was impacting on her.

The guilty feelings and treatment are felt by both, like a game of tennis. When the ball was in my court, I was made to feel selfish and self-centred because of the risks I would take in my quest to be independent again, putting me at risk and not realising the impact it would have on my family. On the other hand, I would throw the ball back into my carer's court, reminding her that they did not care about me. The ideal seemed impractical; it was easier for everyone if I did not overdo things and put myself at risk, causing a problem. That meant doing very little, which was very frustrating and demoralising. This would make it worse for me and, in the long-term, make it bad for everyone. I could imagine myself becoming miserable and bitter and my wife becoming resentful.

I didn't want to be babysat or to be left alone, so it was a no-win situation. I wanted my independence back. I wanted to do so much more: do the garden, DIY, go to the band rehearsals, take on gigs, and generally get out and about. I disliked not being in control of me.

In reality, I couldn't quite do all those things. I had a seizure when I attempted to do the garden on my own. My wife was there to watch over me, so I didn't hurt myself. She had to go out of her way to pick me up from rehearsals in Birmingham because I had a seizure. I was determined to make my own way there, go through the rehearsal and make my way back home, but that didn't quite go according to my plans.

While I was struggling, I couldn't do those things like I used to do. It took so much out of me and left me really needing my wife to do things for me, but I didn't want to ask. This was a tiring, repeating cycle. There are no winners in that game; we both had to learn to adjust and adapt as time went by, with my wife knowing when not to help and me knowing when to ask for help. It does get easier, though.

One thing is for sure: your life is never the same after a near-death experience. There is no longer any fear of death. More emphasis is put on living and celebrating life, holding no grudges, telling loved ones you love them and doing those things you've always wanted to do but never finding the time. We are not here forever, however; I have a few little secrets: live each day like it's your last; there is more enjoyment and satisfaction in giving than receiving; grab your opportunities as they come. Don't wait to live your life. Live it now, within reason. There is so much regret in doing nothing. Attempting to do something and not achieving the desired outcome is not failure, but doing nothing is.

Back to Normal Struggle

I did not consider myself ill. Reality had not kicked in and I tried to do what I would normally have done. One Saturday I got up at noon to make a full English breakfast for the family, as I would have done before.

Del looked at me and said, "Are you sure?"

"Yep," I replied.

I did as much as I could but did not finish; after about thirty minutes, I went back to bed. My legs ached, and I felt light-headed. They call it brain fatigue. I could not concentrate, did not want to talk or think, just needed to lie down. When I did, I must have slept for about four hours. Del had to finish off.

The next challenge was doing a bit of DIY. The blinds in my daughter's room were broken. I could see straight away what the problem was. I got my stepladder and tools out to fix the problem. I climbed up the ladder, leaning towards the broken blinds. They were not that high but, as I climbed, I was so unstable I had to hold the walls to make sure I did not slip off. Determined to prove to myself that I could still do DIY, I got to the fixture that had come undone. I got my screwdriver in my right hand to undo the screw. I did not realise how weak my hand was; I could not make a fist or hold the screwdriver tight. It kept falling out of my hand. In the end, I wedged the fixture under the screw because I did not have the strength to do it.

My last attempt was the boy's bedroom door. It had come off the hinges. I tried as before to put the door back on its hinges, but I could barely hold it, never mind lift it. I gave up. I had to accept defeat. I did not have the strength, cognitive motor skills or coordination to take on this job, so I got my brother to do it.

For the most part, I was always tired and in bed. When I tried to help myself, I ended up overdoing it and spending a lot more time sleeping or resting. A lot of the time I could not think or concentrate through brain fatigue. I learned the hard way not to overdo it.

I would sit in the living room for an hour or so just to get out of the bedroom. My legs were so weak because I spent so much time lying down. Some two weeks later, I got washed and dressed as normal, went downstairs and sat on the corner arm of the settee with my laptop, house phone, and mobile all around me. I felt a sharp pain in my head, right where the tube used to protrude from. I thought nothing of it, putting it down to the healing process. It was the first of a few such occasions. This escalated, and when I felt the sharp pain, there would also be a tremor in my right hand that I could not control, and it would repeat every so often. The whole thing was a constant concern, to the point Del called my local GP to investigate.

Things got worse. My whole body felt hollow. I had no strength. The tremor in my hand was more aggressive, and I became a little unsteady on my feet. I spent more time in bed.

Doctor Examination

When my GP arrived, I was in bed, waiting and very concerned. I accepted that my condition was not getting any better, and in fact, was worse.

"Hello Mr Lewis. How can I help you?" said the doctor.

"Since I have come back from hospital, I keep getting this pain in my head, and my right arm keeps shaking."

"Hmmm. What medication are you taking?"

I told him the whole list of tablets I had to take, including iron tablets, because my blood count was low. He checked my blood pressure, heart rate and iron levels, from what I can remember.

He looked at me with a perturbed look on his face. He could not understand why my blood pressure was low. He was very thorough, and I was grateful for his attention to detail. He noted that there was not enough oxygen in my blood. He called the QE hospital and could not get through. He spent over an hour trying to get more information from my medical records, but without success. In the end, he arranged for me to be admitted to Manor Hospital. I stayed there that night.

The following day we got news back from the QE. They wanted to put me back on the steroids. Straight away, I refused. There was no way I would be popping those pills again, as I remembered the withdrawal symptoms. I suffered for two weeks the last time I came off them. The doctors and nurses tried their best to persuade me to take the wretched tablets, but I would not. I had to take another MRI scan, which needed to be sent off to the QE. I told the Manor staff the only way I would take those tablets was when they managed to get in touch with QE with my MRI results, for them to make a proper assessment. Not even the Manor could get in touch with the QE. The poor nurse tried on and off for the next few hours, with no luck.

By this time, I had fallen asleep. It must have been about four hours later when the Manor hospital was able to communicate with the QE. When they realised the seriousness of my condition I was woken up by a nurse and told I was going to the QE immediately, before I knew it I had Nil-by-mouth put above my bed and a team of paramedics arrived with a stretcher to take me to the QE.
It was late evening by the time I got to the QE. I went in to a bay I had never been in before. I was told that I would go into theatre that night. I didn't actually go in until the following morning. But this is another story written in book two.

Total Shock

Looking back, as I lay in the bed, I believed and was so sure I was healed because I made such a very quick recovery; my eyesight had improved, and I felt great. It was a total shock to me to find myself back in hospital experiencing a relapse. My world stood still; I didn't know what to expect next. This is not how it works when you are healed, not how I understand it from the Bible stories. When you are healed, all sickness is supposed to go and never come back. This was a definite walk of faith. I had to remain optimistic and believe in the prayers, dreams and the word from the Lord that it was already done. Would I live this time around to tell another tale?

When I reflect, after the near-death experience, I was known as 'The Miracle Man' by the many folks who knew me. They did not know how I was going to make it – the odds were against me. They are astounded that not only am I alive and extremely well, but there is hardly any obvious sign that I suffered a stroke induced by a brain tumour the size of a golf ball. The tumour itself was removed.

I was in deep thought while I was physically and emotionally going through this devastating trauma, but in spirit, I was the happiest and most peaceful man alive. I was on cloud nine. When the Lord told me I was valued and I saw the reality of it in the reactions of people towards me, it meant the world. I had peace and calm. It filled me with joy and optimism. This made all the difference to my state of mind.

My Christian upbringing was a good schoolmaster now I needed to put it into practice. My spirit was revived in an instant. My physical body took years to recover from the physical damage, but the hardest part was my soul coming to terms with the whole experience. Did this really happen? Was it a bad dream? Am I going crazy? What do I do now? I had all these questions and feelings to deal with long after the event to keep me focused.

Lao Tzu, the Chinese philosopher, stated, "The journey of a thousand miles begins with a single step." My journey back to life really started in 2010 when my mother passed away and I became seriously ill.

I realise that how I see myself is not necessarily who I am. I need to see me the way God sees me.[7] This was what the Lord was teaching me.

---

[7] "Before I formed thee in the belly I knew thee; and before thou camest forth out of the womb I sanctified thee". A quote from the King James Version of the Bible (1769), excerpt taken from Jeremiah 1:5.

Glossary

Patois. The everyday language of the people of Jamaican origin. It is a combination of English, Spanish, Portuguese, even French with African phrases.

Locked-in syndrome: A neurological disorder characterised by complete paralysis of voluntary muscles in all parts of the body except for those that control eye movement. The locked-in syndrome is usually a complication of a cerebrovascular accident (a stroke) in the base of the pons in the brainstem. The patient is alert and fully conscious but cannot move. Only vertical movements of the eyes and blinking are possible.

Locked-in syndrome can also be due to traumatic brain injury, demyelinating diseases (disorders in which the insulating material around brain cells is lost), and medication overdose.

There is no cure for locked-in syndrome, nor is there a standard course of treatment. Functional neuromuscular stimulation may help activate some paralysed muscles. Several devices to help communication are available. Other treatment is symptomatic and supportive. The prognosis for those with locked-in syndrome is poor. The majority of patients do not regain function.

Fred Plum and Jerome Posner coined the term for this disorder in 1966. Locked-in syndrome is also known as cerebromedullospinal disconnection, de-efferented state, pseudocoma and ventral pontine syndrome.

CT scan: A CT scan is a Computerised Tomography scan. It is a special type of X-ray using a scanner and computer equipment to take pictures of the brain or spine. It differs from a standard X-ray as it produces pictures of cross sections of the brain or spine.

During a scan, patients will be asked to lie on a scanner table. They should mention if they are uncomfortable because it is important they are able to keep still during the scan. When they are comfortable and ready, the staff will leave the room. They will continue to talk with the patient using an intercom.

The scanner table then moves through the scanner to take the first picture. The scanner rotates in small movements around the patient's head to take further pictures. Up to thirty pictures might be taken during one session.

A CT scan is a painless procedure and usually takes twenty minutes or longer.

MRI scan: A Magnetic Resonance Imaging scan. It uses strong magnetic fields and radio waves to take pictures of the brain or spine.

It differs from a standard X-ray, as it produces very detailed pictures of the brain or spine.

Although an MRI scan is painless, unfortunately, the scanner is very noisy. Each set of pictures takes about five minutes, and several sets might be taken during one session. The whole procedure usually takes about forty-five minutes.

Bibliography

Definition of Locked-in syndrome, by:

http://www.medterms.com/script/main/art.asp?articlekey=11024 (1999).

"A journey of a thousand miles begins with a single step." Quote from *The Way of Lao Tzu* attributed to Chinese philosopher Lao Tzu (604 BC–531 BC).

Brain Basics by http://www.brainline.org/multimedia (2012).

Brain and Spine Scans by The Brain and Spine Foundation (2009).

A Dictionary of Scripture Proper Names, by J.B. Jackson (1909).

Afghanistan War:
https://www.britannica.com/event/Afghanistan-War
(accessed, 2020).

War in Afghanistan: https://www.nam.ac.uk/explore/war-afghanistan (accessed, 2020).

September 11 attacks: https//www.history.com/topics/21st-century/9-11-attacks (accessed, 2020).

September 11 attacks: https://www.britannica.com/event/September-11-attacks (accessed, 2020).

About The Author
Irvine 'CalJah' Lewis

Married to Del, for 33 years with four children, brought up in a Pentecostal Church he became a Christian at the age of 17. His hobbies are reading, playing the saxophone and running.

During his musical journey he has played for various gospel artist, choirs, bands, GRP Orchestra, his local church and studio sessions.

By day his profession is a Systems Analyst an I.T. professional who has covered a wide scope of roles in the computer world.

This is Irvine's first published book.

www.marciampublishinghouse.com

Printed in Great Britain
by Amazon